ANTIPOPE CULTURE

The Would-Be Popes, Papal Pretenders & Holy Headaches of Church History

POPE CULTURE SERIES

PAMELA PETTYFEATHER

PETTYFEATHER PUBLISHING

CONTENTS

Part One
ANTIPOPES 101

Part Two
THE ROGUES' GALLERY

Part One
THE EARLY RIVALS

Part Two
THE IMPERIAL PUPPETS

Part Three
THE CHAOTIC MEDIEVALS

Part Four
THE SCHISMATICS

Part Five
THE POST-SCHISM FRINGE

Part Three
WARS OF THE TIARA

Part Four
TRIVIA, TIMELINES & HOLY CHAOS

Part One

ANTIPOPES 101

SO... WHAT'S AN ANTIPOPE?

1.1: THE PAPACY'S SHADOW SIDE

For nearly two thousand years, the Bishop of Rome—also known as the pope, pontiff, or guy-in-white-on-the-balcony—has been the most recognizable face of Catholic leadership. But for much of that history, there's been one small problem:

Sometimes there's more than one.

And the other one? The rival claimant? The spiritual understudy who says, "Actually, I'm the real pope"?

That's an antipope.

He may have been elected by a different faction of cardinals. He may have had the backing of a king, an emperor, or a particularly determined mob. He may have set up shop in Avignon, Pisa, or somewhere even more unexpected.

But the bottom line? He wasn't the pope.

At least, not officially.

1.2: WHAT IS AN ANTIPOPE, ANYWAY?

The Vatican's definition goes something like this:

An antipope is a person who, in opposition to the legitimately elected pope, claims the papacy and gains significant recognition.

In other words: he's not just pretending. He's contesting. And sometimes, he's doing a shockingly good job of it.

Some antipopes held Rome. Some had armies. Some were adored by theologians and heads of state. Others faded into obscurity, were promptly excommunicated, or wound up being tried posthumously in full papal regalia. (Yes, that happened. We'll get there.)

If you're imagining fringe eccentrics shouting from basements, think bigger. These were serious political players. And they made life very complicated for the Church.

1.3: WHO GETS TO BE POPE—AND WHO DOESN'T

Today, popes are chosen in secret conclaves by cardinals, locked inside the Sistine Chapel until white smoke signals a winner. But that's a relatively modern system. For much of papal history, the process was... let's say fluid. And by fluid, I mean wildly unpredictable.

In the early centuries, the people of Rome got a say. So did local nobles. So did emperors. Occasionally, so did whoever could shout the loudest or bring the most soldiers.

Disputed elections were common. Sometimes rival factions of cardinals elected rival popes on the same day. Sometimes an unpopular pope got replaced with someone more agreeable to the ruling powers. And sometimes popes were simply installed by military force—sword first, theology later.

It's no wonder antipopes kept cropping up. The title came with power, land, and spiritual authority. And everyone—from emperors to idealistic reformers—had a reason to want someone "better" on the papal throne.

1.4: WHY DO ANTIPOPES HAPPEN?

It usually comes down to a mix of politics, personality, and papal dysfunction.

Imperial Entanglements

The Holy Roman Emperors had a habit of picking popes they liked—and removing ones they didn't. Unsurprisingly, this led to duplicate popes and decades of confusion.

Disputed Elections

Conclave chaos was a recurring theme. Imagine the Oscars, but two winners are announced, neither is willing to give up the statue, and both have armies.

Reform vs. Tradition

Some antipopes rose up in moments of real crisis, pushing for a more "authentic" Church. Others stood against reform and wanted to bring things back to the good old days (whenever those were).

Real Estate & Revenue

Controlling the papacy meant controlling land, tax income, and military power. That's a lot of incentive to back your own pope, especially if the current one doesn't align with your interests—or your wallet.

1.5: ARE THERE STILL ANTIPOPES?

Technically, yes. The Church stopped recognizing new antipopes after the 15th century, but that hasn't stopped a few determined individuals from claiming the papacy.

In the modern era, breakaway Catholic groups and self-appointed prophets have declared themselves pope from places like Spain, Canada, and the American Midwest. They don't have the armies or empires backing them, but they do have websites, followers, and—in at least one case—papal vestments purchased online.

So while the days of antipopes shaping European politics may be over, the impulse to claim the throne of Peter is alive and well. And occasionally livestreamed.

1.6: WHY THIS BOOK EXISTS

Most history books treat antipopes as footnotes. Asterisks. Names on a disputed timeline.

But these men were far from minor. Some shaped doctrine. Some nearly toppled the Church. Some held power for decades. Others lasted barely a week.

Together, they reveal the messier side of Church history—where legitimacy was negotiated, loyalty was split, and more than a few robes were torn in frustration.

This is their story: the story of the would-be popes, the papal pretenders, and the holy headaches they left behind.

HOW TO BECOME A POPE IN 3 EASY STEPS

(Disclaimer: results may vary. Also, eternal damnation not included.)

So, you've read through 1,800 years of papal drama, theological feuds, and bizarre coronations—and you're thinking, Hey, I could do that.

Here's your three-step crash course in how to become a pope... without the inconvenience of an actual conclave.

STEP 1: DECIDE THE SEAT OF PETER IS EMPTY

The first rule of antipapacy? Claim there is no valid pope.

Maybe the real pope is a heretic. Maybe the Vatican fell to modernism. Maybe the papal chair was secretly transferred to Spain, Kansas, or your garage in Milwaukee.

Don't worry if the Church disagrees. That's kind of the point.

Pro tip: Bonus credibility if you say the last valid pope died decades ago and the Church has been "vacant" ever since. This is called sedevacantism, and it's been the theological framework for most modern antipopes.

STEP 2: GET ELECTED BY AT LEAST ONE PERSON (IDEALLY YOURSELF)

While historical antipopes had cardinals, emperors, or mobs backing them, modern claimants tend to keep it simple.

Some are elected by small groups. Some just declare themselves divinely appointed. One even claimed Jesus personally told him to take over.

If you can find a spare bishop to consecrate you, even better. If not, just start issuing encyclicals and see what happens. The internet makes self-promotion much easier than it used to be.

Pro tip: Vestments are available online. Free shipping if you buy the tiara and crozier together. Also, having a good website helps—medieval antipopes would have killed for a WordPress blog.

STEP 3: SET UP SHOP SOMEWHERE WITH RELIABLE WI-FI

Gone are the days of storming Rome with mercenaries. Today's antipopes operate from farmhouses, bunkers, or modest suburban homes—anywhere you can livestream a papal blessing and post declarations of excommunication.

Start a website. Build a YouTube channel. Canonize your great-aunt. Issue bulls about the proper length of altar cloths.

Congratulations: you're the pope now. At least to a dozen people—and one confused Reddit thread.

Pro tip: Don't forget the Latin. Or at least the Google Translate version of it. Papal pronouncements sound more official in Latin, even if your grammar is questionable.

FINAL NOTE:

If this all sounds too easy, remember: most antipopes end up forgotten, imprisoned, excommunicated, or lovingly mocked in books like this one.

Still tempted?

Try canonizing yourself first.

Baby steps.

Part Two

THE ROGUES' GALLERY

Part One

THE EARLY RIVALS

(1st–5th centuries)

Before there were palaces, armies, and Vatican politics, there were theological arguments—often very personal ones. The first antipopes weren't installed by emperors or crowned in defiance. They rose from within the early Church, staking claims on matters of doctrine, discipline, and forgiveness.

In an age when Christianity itself was illegal, these rival claimants argued about penance for sinners, the nature of the Trinity, and how rigid the Church should be in enforcing orthodoxy. The splits were often local, but the consequences were lasting. Some of these men—like Hippolytus—were respected theologians who ended up reconciled with the very Church they opposed. Others, like Novatian, founded whole sects that survived for decades.

This was the age before papal supremacy was clearly defined. Before conclaves. Before tiaras. The title of pope was still emerging, and so were the boundaries of heresy. In that murky space, the first antipopes stepped forward—half reformers, half rebels, all passionately convinced they were right.

HIPPOLYTUS

Years active: c. 217–235

Rival pope: Callixtus I

Claim to fame: The first official antipope in Church history—and later a saint.

If you're going to be the Church's first major rebel, you might as well go big. Hippolytus was a respected Roman priest, a brilliant theologian, and a man deeply unimpressed with the new pope, Callixtus I. The core of the dispute? Mercy.

Callixtus, elected in 217, had the audacity to forgive sinners. Adulterers, fornicators, murderers—he welcomed them back into the Church after penance. Hippolytus thought this was a moral collapse. He viewed Callixtus as dangerously soft, maybe even heretical.

So Hippolytus didn't just write complaints. He set up his own rival community and declared himself pope.

For nearly two decades, he functioned as a kind of shadow pontiff—writing vigorously, drawing followers, and clashing with successive popes over theology and Church discipline. It was a stubborn, prolonged schism.

Then came a surprise ending. Both Hippolytus and Pope Pontian (Callixtus's later successor) were arrested during a wave of persecution and sent to the mines in Sardinia. Facing death together, they reconciled.

OUTCOME

Hippolytus laid down his claim, made peace with the Church—and eventually became a canonized saint. Today, he's recognized as the first antipope and one of the Church's martyrs. A complicated legacy, but a memorable one.

FUN FACT

Some of the earliest Christian commentary on the Antichrist comes from Hippolytus's writings. Even in exile, he kept the pen moving. He and Pope Pontian share a feast day on August 13—the only antipope ever honored on the Church calendar.

NOVATIAN

Years active: 251–258

Rival pope: Cornelius

Claim to fame: The purist who wouldn't forgive—and found followers who agreed.

After the Decian persecution in 250, the early Church faced a pressing moral question: what to do with the Christians who had denied their faith under pressure? Pope Cornelius took a pastoral approach: allow them to return after penance. Novatian, a Roman priest and gifted theologian, said absolutely not.

In Novatian's view, anyone who had lapsed under persecution had forfeited the right to rejoin the Church. To prove his point, he got himself elected as a rival pope by a small but determined group of clergy.

This was no personal vendetta—it was a theological crusade. Novatian's movement, sometimes called the Novatianists, insisted on an uncompromisingly pure Church. They rejected what they saw as moral leniency and refused to accept that forgiveness could be granted by bishops at all.

Rome, unsurprisingly, did not agree.

Cornelius excommunicated Novatian, and the schism widened. Novatian continued to lead his community independently, gaining followers across the Roman Empire. Even after his death, his sect endured for over a century.

OUTCOME

Novatian was never reconciled with the Church. But his ideas—especially the debate over penance and purity—echoed in later controversies.

FUN FACT

Novatian is sometimes called the first antipope with a manifesto. He wrote extensively, and several of his works survived, including treatises on the Trinity and martyrdom. Ironically, his theological writings were so solid that some later Church fathers quoted them—just not under his name.

FELIX II

Years active: 355–365

Rival pope: Liberius

Claim to fame: The imperial appointee who got swept up in the Arian controversy.

Felix II wasn't elected by the Church. He was installed by the emperor.

In the mid-4th century, the Arian controversy was tearing through Christianity like wildfire. Emperor Constantius II—who leaned heavily toward Arian theology—exiled Pope Liberius, who had refused to condemn the anti-Arian Athanasius. With Liberius out of the way, the emperor handpicked Felix to replace him.

It did not go well.

While some clergy in Rome accepted Felix, most laypeople did not. Crowds rallied behind the exiled Liberius, and resistance to Felix's legitimacy only grew. When Liberius returned from exile in 357, Rome welcomed him like a hero—and Felix was forced into a kind of papal retirement.

Some sources suggest they may have even co-reigned awkwardly for a time, though modern historians aren't convinced. What's clear is that Felix's claim never fully stuck, and the Church does not count him as a valid pope.

OUTCOME

Felix was later honored by some as a confessor and martyr—but the official Vatican list classifies him as an antipope. His tomb was long venerated, and for centuries there was confusion about whether he was a saint. He isn't. The veneration likely stemmed from confusion with an actual Saint Felix.

FUN FACT

Felix II is sometimes listed as "Pope Felix II" in older documents, which caused a numbering headache. As a result, the next real Pope Felix was styled Felix III—even though he was technically only the second. The Vatican basically counted an antipope in the official numbering by accident, and nobody bothered to fix it for over a thousand years.

URSINUS

Years active: 366–367

Rival pope: Damasus I

Claim to fame: The antipope whose supporters turned the election into a bloodbath.

When Pope Liberius died in 366, the Roman Church did what it often did in the fourth century: it held a highly contested, deeply political election. One faction backed Damasus, a seasoned deacon with strong support from the Roman elite. Another backed Ursinus, a deacon whose popularity stemmed from his close association with the late Liberius.

Then things got violent.

Both men were elected pope—on the same day. Riots broke out in the streets. Churches became battlegrounds. Supporters of Damasus reportedly stormed the Basilica of St. Mary Major, killing more than a hundred of Ursinus's followers in a single day. It was less "papal election" and more "urban warfare with bishops."

Eventually, imperial authorities intervened and ruled in favor of Damasus. Ursinus was exiled, though he continued to challenge Damasus's legitimacy from afar, writing letters and rallying sympathy. His schism lingered for years, though he never regained a foothold in Rome.

OUTCOME

Ursinus was ultimately sidelined, but his story illustrates how dangerously high the stakes of papal elections had become. Damasus, for his part, went on to have a long reign—and a suspiciously clean historical record considering how much blood was spilled on his behalf.

FUN FACT

The "Liberian" faction, from which Ursinus emerged, likely represented a more populist wing of the Church. Damasus's victory helped cement the alignment between the papacy and Rome's social and political elite. Some historians argue that Ursinus had the better electoral case—he just lost the street fight.

EULALIUS

Years active: 418–419

Rival pope: Boniface I

Claim to fame: The antipope who almost won—until he annoyed the emperor.

When Pope Zosimus died in 418, Rome once again descended into electoral confusion. Two candidates emerged: Boniface, backed by a strong faction of clergy, and Eulalius, who had the support of the urban prefect and, initially, the emperor Honorius.

Both were consecrated. Both claimed the papacy. The Church was, once again, in schism.

At first, things looked good for Eulalius. With imperial support, he held Rome while Boniface waited in exile. But then Eulalius made a mistake: he defied an imperial order and attempted to celebrate Easter Mass at the Lateran Basilica—Rome's oldest and most important church—without permission.

The emperor wasn't amused. He switched his support to Boniface, and Eulalius was swiftly banished from the city.

OUTCOME

Boniface I reigned in peace. Eulalius vanished from the historical record. His candidacy, though brief, marks one of the clearest examples of just how decisive imperial favor could be—until you lost it.

FUN FACT

Eulalius is considered one of the last "imperial antipopes" of the early Church era—a reminder that, for much of Church history, secular rulers had just as much say in papal politics as cardinals did. Also, never defy an emperor's direct order when he's the only reason you're pope.

Part Two

THE IMPERIAL PUPPETS

(6th–9th centuries)

As Christianity spread and became the state religion of the Roman Empire, a new dynamic emerged: popes became political players, and emperors wanted in on the action. In this era, antipopes were rarely elected—they were installed.

These were the years of Byzantine interference, Lombard invasions, and the slow emergence of the Holy Roman Empire. Emperors in Constantinople or Aachen saw the papacy as another bishopric to control. When the sitting pope proved inconvenient, they simply appointed someone else—and called him pope.

These antipopes were often short-lived, swept in and out of power by shifting alliances. But their presence reveals just how fragile papal authority was. The office wasn't yet sacred. It was still very much up for grabs—and whoever had the army often won.

This section features men caught between swords and sacraments, sometimes pawns, sometimes willing collaborators in the imperial game. Their stories remind us that for centuries, the papacy was anything but independent.

LAURENTIUS

Years active: 498–506

Rival pope: Symmachus

Claim to fame: The schism that forced Theodoric the Ostrogoth to play referee.

The death of Pope Anastasius II sparked yet another disputed papal election. This time, the division was partly about theology—and partly about politics.

On one side stood Symmachus, elected by the majority of Roman clergy. On the other stood Laurentius, backed by a minority of clerics but supported by a strong faction of Roman aristocrats.

Both men were consecrated pope. Cue chaos.

Theodoric the Great, the Ostrogothic king of Italy, was called in to settle the matter. A pagan ruler presiding over a Christian dispute, Theodoric initially sided with Symmachus—probably because he was elected first. But the situation didn't end there.

Laurentius remained a powerful figure in Rome, and for years the city was effectively divided between his supporters and Symmachus's.

Accusations of bribery, simony, and violence filled the air. At one point, Symmachus was even accused of fleeing the city during Lent to avoid being tried for misconduct.

Eventually, Laurentius was persuaded—perhaps forced—to withdraw. Symmachus retained the title. But the schism cast a long shadow.

OUTCOME

Laurentius was never formally condemned but quietly faded from Church life. Symmachus remained pope, though his reign was deeply controversial.

FUN FACT

This episode helped prompt the eventual development of stricter election rules for popes. If nothing else, Rome had grown tired of dual papacies. Also, having a pagan king settle your papal dispute is not a great look for institutional authority.

DIOSCORUS

Years active: 530 (22 days)

Rival pope: Boniface II

Claim to fame: The antipope who died before anyone could figure out if he was legitimate.

When Pope Felix IV died in 530, Rome faced yet another disputed succession. Felix had nominated his own successor—Boniface—but a significant faction of clergy rejected this irregular appointment and quickly elected their own candidate: Dioscorus, a Greek deacon.

Both men were consecrated on the same day. Both claimed the papacy. But before the dispute could escalate into full schism, Dioscorus died—just 22 days after his election.

With Dioscorus gone, Boniface II assumed the papacy without further contest. But even then, controversy lingered. Boniface attempted to force the Roman clergy to anathematize Dioscorus posthumously, which many resisted. The whole affair left a bitter taste.

Some historians argue that Dioscorus may have had the stronger canonical claim, since Felix IV's attempt to nominate his own successor violated traditional election procedures. But with Dioscorus's sudden death, the question became moot.

OUTCOME

Dioscorus is listed as an antipope, though his legitimacy remains debated. His brief papacy highlights how murky the line between pope and antipope could be in the sixth century.

FUN FACT

Dioscorus is one of the shortest-reigning antipopes in history. His 22-day papacy barely gave him time to settle into the Lateran—let alone issue any decrees. Some scholars suspect he may have been poisoned, but evidence is non-existent. In the end, he's remembered mostly for what he didn't have time to do.

THEODORE

Year active: 687

Rival pope: Sergius I

Claim to fame: One of three claimants to the papacy during a chaotic Roman election—with imperial politics looming large.

In 687, the papal election turned into something closer to a traffic jam. Pope Conon had died, and three factions emerged, each with its own preferred candidate. The result? A rare—and thoroughly confusing—three-way schism. Theodore, a respected archpriest, was one of the contenders.

The Roman clergy was deeply divided. Some rallied behind Paschal, an ambitious archdeacon. Others, wary of Paschal's imperial connections and Theodore's Roman power base, sought a compromise in Sergius, another senior priest. The city quickly fractured, and all three candidates had themselves proclaimed pope—though none through a properly convened election.

Theodore's supporters briefly secured a few Roman churches and tried to establish legitimacy, but the tides turned fast. Paschal was caught conspiring with the Byzantine exarch of Ravenna—an imperial official

—prompting a backlash. And as the dust settled, Sergius gained traction as the least controversial option.

By the time the real electors managed to regroup, Theodore had been quietly sidelined. Sergius was consecrated as pope, with widespread recognition. Theodore faded into obscurity shortly thereafter—no rebellion, no martyrdom, no counter-campaign. Just a dignified exit from a particularly confusing page in papal succession.

OUTCOME

Theodore's claim was brief and mostly political, driven more by local ambition than theological dispute. He left no writings and led no movement. But his inclusion on official antipope lists highlights just how chaotic and improvisational papal elections could be in the 7th century.

FUN FACT

The papal succession crisis of 687 directly influenced future reforms to election procedure. The three-candidate debacle made it clear that the Church needed more guardrails—and fewer noble families trying to stage-manage the process. Also, Theodore and Paschal are sometimes confused in historical records, which is fitting for a year when nobody could agree on anything.

PASCHAL

Year active: 687

Rival pope: Sergius I

Claim to fame: The imperial-backed antipope who tried to buy the papacy—and failed spectacularly.

While Theodore had local Roman support during the 687 papal crisis, Paschal took a different approach: he cut a deal with the Byzantine exarch of Ravenna, promising money and favors in exchange for military backing.

It almost worked. With imperial troops at his disposal, Paschal seized several key basilicas in Rome and had himself declared pope. For a moment, it looked like he might succeed through sheer force.

But his conspiracy came to light. When the Roman clergy and people learned that Paschal had essentially tried to purchase the papacy with bribes to Byzantine officials, support evaporated. The exarch's forces withdrew, and Paschal's claim collapsed.

The victorious Pope Sergius I dealt with him mercifully—rather than execution or exile, Paschal was confined to a monastery, where he lived out his days in obscurity.

OUTCOME

Paschal's attempted simony became a cautionary tale. His failed bid helped crystallize opposition to imperial interference in papal elections and strengthened calls for reform.

FUN FACT

Paschal is sometimes listed as "Antipope Paschal" or "Paschal I (antipope)" to distinguish him from the later legitimate Pope Paschal I (817-824). The confusion has led to centuries of papal historians double-checking their notes. Also, trying to bribe Byzantine officials to make you pope is a bold strategy—but apparently not a winning one.

CONSTANTINE II

Years active: 767–768

Rival pope: Stephen III

Claim to fame: Installed by armed force, ordained through all church ranks in a matter of days, and quickly ousted in one of Rome's most lawless papal moments.

Constantine II may be one of the most flagrantly illegitimate antipopes in Church history—but that didn't stop him from getting the job. Following the death of Pope Paul I in 767, the papacy was up for grabs. And the powerful Roman noble Duke Toto of Nepi had someone in mind: his brother, Constantine.

There was just one problem. Constantine wasn't a bishop. Or a priest. Or even a deacon. He was a layman—an educated one, yes, but nowhere near canonically qualified to lead the Church.

Toto solved this by having Constantine ordained through all necessary clerical ranks in under a week—a marathon sprint through the ecclesiastical ladder. Backed by armed forces, the brothers secured the Lateran, held an irregular election, and crowned Constantine pope.

For about a year, Constantine ruled Rome as a usurper. He styled himself as a legitimate pontiff, issued decrees, and tried to stabilize his position through bribes and noble alliances. But opposition grew. A rival group appealed to the Frankish king and began organizing resistance.

Eventually, Stephen, a more canonically acceptable candidate, was elected with external support. Constantine was forcibly removed from the papal palace, imprisoned, and reportedly blinded—a brutal but not uncommon punishment for illegitimate claimants.

OUTCOME

Constantine was never recognized by the broader Church and left no theological legacy. His rule is remembered mostly as a cautionary tale about just how far noble families would go to control the papacy—and how violently the system could self-correct.

FUN FACT

Because of the irregularity of Constantine's ordination, some sources don't list him as a valid cleric at all—meaning he may have been the only "pope" in history to hold the office without ever being truly eligible for holy orders. Also, his blinding and imprisonment inspired the Lateran Council of 769, which established new rules to prevent laymen from seizing the papacy. So at least something good came from the chaos.

PHILIP

YEAR ACTIVE: 768 (ONE DAY)

RIVAL POPE: STEPHEN III

CLAIM TO FAME: THE ONE-DAY POPE WHO WENT BACK TO HIS MONASTERY.

After Constantine II was violently deposed in 768, there was a brief moment of confusion before Stephen III could be properly elected. During that window, a priest named Philip was proclaimed pope—possibly by Lombard forces, possibly by confused Roman clergy, possibly by accident. Historical sources disagree.

What's clear is that Philip's papacy lasted approximately one day. He was installed in the morning, and by evening—either through his own choice or through pressure—he renounced the claim and returned to his monastery.

Some accounts suggest Philip was reluctant from the start and only accepted the role under duress. Others hint that he saw the writing on the wall: with Constantine's supporters crushed and Stephen's faction gaining strength, there was no path forward.

Either way, Philip quietly exited papal history as quickly as he'd entered it.

OUTCOME

Philip is sometimes omitted from antipope lists entirely due to his extremely brief tenure and unclear circumstances. But most historians count him, if only as a footnote to the chaos of 768.

FUN FACT

Philip holds the distinction of being one of the shortest-reigning papal claimants in history—possibly the shortest, depending on how you count. He's also one of the few who seems to have voluntarily walked away without being imprisoned, exiled, or executed. Smart man.

JOHN VIII

Year active: 844

Rival pope: Sergius II

Claim to fame: Briefly backed by a Roman faction during a contested election—until Sergius II's supporters physically removed him from power.

The death of Pope Gregory IV in 844 unleashed one of those swift, politically charged succession crises that had become increasingly common in Rome. The moment the pope died, factions in the city sprang into action—not to mourn, but to campaign.

One faction, made up largely of Roman nobility, quickly threw its support behind John, a respected deacon. They saw him as a local candidate who could keep Rome's elite in the loop and maintain the delicate balance between imperial influence and native control.

But they weren't the only ones acting fast. Another group of clergy and officials maneuvered to install Sergius II, a more established cleric with broad Church support. As both factions moved to claim the Lateran, Sergius's supporters gained the upper hand—literally.

John was physically ejected from the basilica, and Sergius was consecrated before imperial approval could even arrive. The whole episode lasted just days, but it was intense enough to make its mark in papal history.

Afterward, Sergius worked to consolidate power and soothe tensions with the Holy Roman Emperor Lothair I. John, meanwhile, disappears from the record—no follow-up rebellion, no excommunication, no reinstatement attempt. Just a failed claim and a very short-lived papacy.

OUTCOME

John's papal bid was brief and local. He's considered an antipope only because he was publicly declared pope by a faction, not because he ever posed a serious challenge to Sergius's legitimacy.

FUN FACT

The antipope John of 844 has often been confused with Pope John VIII (872–882), a far more influential figure. This mix-up muddled Church records for centuries—and probably didn't help the poor antipope's reputation. Being forgotten is one thing; being mistaken for someone else entirely is another.

ANASTASIUS BIBLIOTHECARIUS

Year active: 855

Rival pope: Benedict III

Claim to fame: The scholar-antipope who tried to seize the papacy—and was excommunicated for his trouble.

Anastasius was no ordinary antipope. Before his ill-fated papal bid, he was one of the most learned men in Rome—a librarian, theologian, and translator who had access to the Church's most important manuscripts. He was also ambitious.

When Pope Leo IV died in 855, there was brief confusion about the succession. Benedict, a respected priest, was the clear favorite. But a faction of Roman nobles—backed by Emperor Louis II—decided to install Anastasius instead, bypassing the normal electoral process.

Anastasius was enthroned by force and held the Lateran for a matter of days. But the Roman clergy and people rejected him. Benedict's supporters rallied, and with popular backing, they drove Anastasius out of Rome.

Benedict III was consecrated as the legitimate pope, and Anastasius was formally excommunicated. Remarkably, he was later rehabilitated —his scholarly reputation was too valuable to waste. He returned to Rome, served as a papal librarian again, and even helped with important translations. But his papal ambitions were over.

OUTCOME

Anastasius Bibliothecarius is one of the few antipopes who managed to have a successful career after his failed bid for the papacy. His scholarly work survived, even if his political gamble didn't.

FUN FACT

Anastasius translated Greek theological texts into Latin, making Byzantine scholarship accessible to the Western Church. He's sometimes called "the most learned man of his age"—which makes his decision to try seizing the papacy all the more baffling. Apparently even brilliant scholars can make terrible political choices. Also, "Bibliothecarius" literally means "librarian," which is possibly the most endearing title any antipope has ever had.

CHRISTOPHER

Years active: 903–904

Rival pope: Leo V (disputed)

Claim to fame: Possibly an antipope, possibly a pope—depending on which Church history you ask.

The case of Christopher is less "rebellious uprising" and more "shadowy succession." In 903, Pope Leo V was briefly elected to the papacy, but his reign ended almost immediately under mysterious circumstances. Some sources suggest he was deposed by force. Others say he was imprisoned. A few imply he was murdered. All agree that Christopher appeared very soon afterward—and claimed the papal throne for himself.

Whether Christopher was elected, acclaimed, or simply seized power is unclear. What is clear is that he reigned for several months, acted as pope, and appears in some early papal lists as a legitimate pontiff. He issued documents, celebrated Mass at St. Peter's, and conducted the affairs of the Church.

Then came Sergius III, a rival with powerful backers and his own ambitions. Sergius returned to Rome, deposed Christopher, and took the papal throne. According to later chronicles, Christopher was imprisoned and possibly strangled to death.

And then things got confusing.

For centuries, some lists included Christopher as Pope Christopher I, while others branded him an antipope. Today, the Vatican omits him from the official roster of popes, but historians remain divided. Was he a usurper? A placeholder? A reformer? Or simply an unfortunate political victim in an especially murky year?

OUTCOME

Though widely treated as an antipope today, Christopher's brief rule straddled the line between contested authority and de facto papacy. His ambiguous legacy continues to spark debate among Church historians.

FUN FACT

Christopher's uncertain status has made him a litmus test for how different eras define legitimacy. His case highlights how thin the line could be between pope and antipope in the 10th century—especially when the documentation was, at best, spotty. Also, dying in prison without a clear verdict on your papacy is perhaps the worst possible legacy for a Church leader.

Part Three

THE CHAOTIC MEDIEVALS

(10th–13th centuries)

The Middle Ages brought the papacy to full political power—and with it, full-blown chaos. Popes were elected in backrooms, bribed into office, and occasionally thrown off balconies. Noble families turned Rome into a turf war. Cardinals took bribes. Crowds rioted. And emperors kept meddling.

This was the age of violent elections and long grudges. The line between pope and antipope wasn't just blurred—it was often decided by who had the keys to the Lateran Basilica on any given morning.

Some antipopes in this era held power for years, functioned like real popes, and were only deemed "anti" later. Others were ousted in days. What they shared was a backdrop of intense political instability—where loyalty often mattered more than theology, and any papal rival with enough noble or imperial backing had a real shot.

This is the most unpredictable category: part gangland, part reform movement, part ecclesiastical brawl. The chaotic medievals didn't just claim the throne—they fought for it.

BONIFACE VII

Years active: 974, 984–985

Rival popes: Benedict VI, John XIV

Claim to fame: Twice a usurper, excommunicated even after death, and widely regarded as one of the most corrupt figures in papal history.

Where many antipopes were theologians or reformers with questionable claims, Boniface VII was something else entirely: a ruthless political operator with few scruples and fewer friends. His first grab for the papacy came in 974 when he led a faction that overthrew and imprisoned Pope Benedict VI, who was later found strangled in his cell.

Boniface installed himself as pope—without election—and reigned for just a few months before he was forced to flee Rome with the Church treasury. He spent nearly a decade in exile in Constantinople, biding his time.

In 984, he returned to Rome with a vengeance. This time he had military support and a vendetta. He captured Pope John XIV, imprisoned him in the Castel Sant'Angelo, and may have ordered his death as well.

Once again, Boniface seized the papacy and ruled as a tyrant—this time for nearly a year.

Rome, however, had no affection for him. His reputation for violence, greed, and vindictiveness alienated both the clergy and the public. When he died suddenly in 985 (possibly poisoned), the city erupted in celebration. His corpse was dragged through the streets and left beneath a statue.

OUTCOME

Boniface VII was condemned posthumously and written off as a usurper by nearly every ecclesiastical source. His reigns—both of them—are remembered not for doctrinal disputes but for murder, bribery, and raw political power.

FUN FACT

Boniface VII's reputation was so toxic that even the later, scandal-ridden Renaissance popes avoided taking the name Boniface. It remained tainted for centuries. Also, having your corpse dragged through the streets is perhaps the ultimate sign that your papacy didn't go well.

JOHN XVI

Years active: 997–998

Rival pope: Gregory V

Claim to fame: Installed by Byzantine support, brutally punished, and remembered as one of the most viciously treated antipopes in history.

John XVI's story is one of power politics, imperial meddling, and a particularly grim ending. A Greek cleric from Calabria, John was the trusted secretary of the powerful Crescentii family—one of the leading noble dynasties in Rome. When Pope Gregory V (a German noble and the first pope appointed by Otto III, Holy Roman Emperor) fell out of favor with the Roman elite, the Crescentii staged a coup.

With the backing of Byzantine Emperor Basil II, they installed John as pope in 997.

John's claim was purely political. He was seen as a pro-Byzantine counterweight to the German emperor's influence. But his reign didn't last long. Otto III returned to Rome in force, Gregory V was restored, and John XVI was captured while trying to flee.

What followed was unusually brutal—even by medieval standards. John was tortured, had his nose and ears cut off, his tongue removed, and his eyes gouged out. Then he was paraded through Rome on a donkey, facing backward, as a public humiliation. It was a calculated spectacle meant to send a message: this is what happens to pretenders.

Miraculously, he survived. After his public disgrace, he was sent to a monastery, where he lived out the remainder of his life in obscurity.

OUTCOME

John XVI's reign lasted barely a year, but his downfall became infamous. His brutal treatment, widely recorded by chroniclers, stood in contrast to his relatively mild papal activity. In the end, he was a political pawn who paid the full price of rebellion.

FUN FACT

Despite being an antipope, John XVI was not the sixteenth pope by that name. The real Pope John XV had reigned earlier, but due to confusion and double-counting in the medieval papal registry, the next legitimate John became John XVII—skipping XVI entirely. So John XVI exists in the numbering gap created by medieval record-keeping chaos.

GREGORY

Year active: 1012

Rival pope: Benedict VIII

Claim to fame: A brief imperial-backed challenge that fizzled almost immediately.

When Benedict VIII was elected pope in 1012, not everyone was on board. A faction of Roman nobles, dissatisfied with the choice and looking to assert their own influence, quickly elevated their own candidate—a Roman priest named Gregory.

Gregory was backed by the powerful Crescentii family, the same dynasty that had supported John XVI a decade earlier. They installed Gregory with the hope of controlling papal politics, but this time the plan fell apart almost immediately.

Benedict VIII had strong support from the German emperor Henry II, and more importantly, he had popular backing in Rome. Gregory's claim was purely political, lacking both theological justification and widespread recognition. Within weeks—possibly even days—Gregory's position collapsed.

He was driven from Rome and disappears from the historical record without much fanfare. No dramatic imprisonment, no public humiliation, no martyrdom. Just a quiet exit from a very short papacy.

OUTCOME

Gregory's antipapacy was so brief and inconsequential that some papal lists forget to include him entirely. He's remembered mainly as evidence that by the 11th century, simply having noble backing wasn't enough—you needed broader support.

FUN FACT

Gregory is sometimes called "the forgotten antipope" because he made so little impact. His brief challenge to Benedict VIII is mostly notable for how quickly it failed. Also, the Crescentii family's track record with antipopes was not great—0 for 2 by this point.

BENEDICT X

Years active: 1058–1059

Rival pope: Nicholas II

Claim to fame: Elected under pressure from Roman nobles—deposed by reformers pushing for papal independence from aristocratic influence.

Benedict X wasn't an obscure cleric or self-proclaimed visionary—he was part of the powerful Tusculan family, long embedded in the political life of Rome. When Pope Stephen IX died in 1058, a faction of Roman aristocrats rushed to fill the power vacuum. Before reform-minded cardinals could even organize a conclave, Benedict—born Giovanni Mincio—was hastily elected and consecrated.

The problem? The election violated Church procedure and lacked broad support among reformers, especially those aligned with Hildebrand (the future Pope Gregory VII), who was then the rising power in the curia. The reformers fled Rome and convened their own council, eventually electing Nicholas II as the legitimate pope.

Backed by Norman forces from southern Italy, Nicholas returned to Rome in force. Benedict X was driven from the city, excommunicated, and eventually captured. He was deposed in 1059 and forced to formally renounce his claim.

What followed wasn't merely a change in personnel—it was a change in policy. Nicholas II enacted sweeping electoral reforms that drastically limited the influence of Roman nobility on papal elections and strengthened the authority of the College of Cardinals.

OUTCOME

Benedict X spent the rest of his life in monastic confinement. His brief papacy—officially declared illegitimate—became a key turning point in the battle between secular control and Church autonomy.

FUN FACT

For centuries, Benedict X was listed as a legitimate pope. It wasn't until later reforms clarified his illegitimacy that papal numbering was adjusted—meaning that Benedict XI was actually only the tenth valid Benedict. The confusion lasted so long that some medieval manuscripts still count Benedict X as real.

HONORIUS II

Years active: 1061–1064

Rival pope: Alexander II

Claim to fame: Backed by German imperial authorities during a tense standoff between secular rulers and Church reformers.

Not to be confused with the later, legitimate Pope Honorius II, this Honorius was the antipope caught in the middle of a theological tug-of-war between imperial power and reformist momentum.

After Pope Nicholas II died in 1061, reformers in Rome quickly elected Alexander II—a candidate associated with Hildebrand and the growing movement to liberate the Church from secular influence. However, the Holy Roman Emperor's regent, Empress Agnes of Poitou, didn't approve.

In response, a synod in Basel—convened by imperial loyalists—elected Bishop Cadalus of Parma, who took the name Honorius II. Backed by military support, Honorius marched on Rome and even gained control of parts of the city. For three years, the two men claimed the papacy simultaneously.

Honorius's reign was serious and well-funded, and he made a strong legal case for imperial involvement in Church affairs. But momentum gradually shifted toward Alexander II. A decisive Roman synod, backed by increasing Norman support and the future Pope Gregory VII, ruled in Alexander's favor.

By 1064, Honorius's claims had collapsed. He returned to Parma, where he continued to assert his right to the papacy in writing—but not in practice.

OUTCOME

Honorius II's schism signaled the beginning of the Investiture Controversy, the larger battle over who controlled the appointment of Church officials. Though he failed to hold Rome, his conflict set the stage for one of the most defining struggles of the medieval Church.

FUN FACT

Because his name was later taken by a legitimate pope, the historical record of Honorius II (antipope) is often confused, collapsed, or overlooked—despite the serious implications of his rebellion. Medieval scribes sometimes had to write "Honorius II (the false one)" in the margins to keep track.

CLEMENT III

Years active: 1080–1100

Rival pope: Gregory VII, then successors

Claim to fame: Longest-reigning antipope, installed by Emperor Henry IV during the height of the Investiture Controversy.

If antipapacy were a career track, Clement III would be the model of longevity. Born Wibert of Ravenna, he was a canon and imperial loyalist who rose through the Church ranks thanks to his loyalty to the German emperor, Henry IV.

When Pope Gregory VII excommunicated Henry IV over lay investiture (the practice of secular rulers appointing bishops), Henry responded with force. In 1080, he appointed Wibert as his pope of choice—Clement III—and marched on Rome.

Gregory VII was driven into exile, and Clement was installed in St. Peter's. He even presided over Henry's coronation as Holy Roman Emperor in 1084. Though Clement was never recognized by the reform-minded Church, his rule lasted two decades—far longer than most antipopes, and long after Gregory VII died in exile.

Clement III held court in Rome intermittently, depending on which faction held the city. He functioned as a real rival pope, appointing bishops, issuing decrees, and attracting followers among those loyal to the emperor. Several of his antipapal successors continued the line until 1111.

OUTCOME

Clement's death in 1100 marked the end of the strongest phase of imperial antipapacy. His reign—propped up by secular force—became a case study in what happens when Church and state enter open war.

FUN FACT

Clement was anathematized more than once, but his ecclesiastical acts were so widespread that later popes had to quietly confirm or reassign many of the bishops he'd named. Even an antipope's paperwork leaves a trail. Also, lasting 20 years as an antipope is impressive—most couldn't make it 20 months.

THEODORIC

Year active: 1100–1101

Rival pope: Paschal II

Claim to fame: The short-lived successor to Clement III, whose antipapacy lasted less than a year and ended in obscurity.

Following the death of Clement III in 1100, the imperial-aligned faction in Rome didn't give up their fight. Though Clement's influence had been declining, his supporters weren't ready to cede ground to Paschal II, the reigning pope recognized by the broader Church. In a bid to continue their challenge, they elected a new antipope: Theodoric, a cardinal and staunch ally of the imperial cause.

But momentum was no longer on their side. The Norman-backed forces supporting Paschal II had grown stronger, and the appetite for more schism among the Roman populace had worn thin after two decades of conflict. Theodoric never gained widespread recognition, and his time in Rome was brief.

Within months of his elevation, Theodoric was captured by Paschal's supporters, publicly humiliated, and sent into exile. Some sources say he was imprisoned in a monastery; others suggest he voluntarily retired from public life. Either way, his papacy ended without much resistance —or much legacy.

OUTCOME

Theodoric's antipapacy was mostly symbolic, a transitional figure for the remnants of Clement III's movement. With no strong political backing or enduring vision, his claim quickly collapsed.

FUN FACT

Theodoric's fleeting rule was so underwhelming that many papal chronologies forget to include him. Even among antipopes, his obscurity is notable. He's the ecclesiastical equivalent of a footnote to a footnote.

ADALBERT

Year active: 1101

Rival pope: Paschal II

Claim to fame: Possibly elected, possibly fabricated—Adalbert may be the least documented antipope in Church history.

If Theodoric was a footnote, Adalbert is more of a ghost. Mentioned in only a handful of sources, Adalbert was allegedly elected by the same faction that had supported Clement III and Theodoric—suggesting a desperate effort to keep the antipapal momentum alive.

His name appears in some 12th-century chronicles as a briefly declared antipope, but with no specific records of his actions, location, or supporters. There are no surviving papal bulls, no decrees, no signs of governance. In fact, it's unclear whether he was ever consecrated, or if his "election" was more of a protest gesture than a serious bid for the throne.

What little we know suggests he may have been a Roman cardinal, possibly aligned with the last remnants of the imperial faction. But even that is speculation. Modern historians debate whether Adalbert was an actual antipope or simply a later invention—possibly confused with another cleric or inserted to explain a gap in the anti-Gregorian succession.

If he did exist, his papacy was measured in weeks, not months. He made no lasting impact on Church governance, issued no known documents, and left behind no followers. By early 1102, the imperial antipope line had effectively ended, and Adalbert—if he was ever real—vanished with it.

OUTCOME

Assuming he existed, Adalbert held the title of antipope for a matter of weeks or months. He had no impact on Church governance and left no meaningful legacy. His inclusion on some antipope lists seems to be based more on completeness than actual evidence.

FUN FACT

Some historians think Adalbert's story may have originated from a scribal error or a case of mistaken identity—making him possibly the only antipope created by accident. Either that, or he's the most successfully forgotten man in papal history. Being so obscure that people debate whether you existed is a special kind of historical erasure.

SYLVESTER IV

Years active: 1105–1111

Rival pope: Paschal II

Claim to fame: The last serious imperial antipope—crowned during a final push by Roman nobles to reclaim influence over the papacy.

By 1105, Paschal II had been pope for nearly a decade and was doing his best to steer the Church through the final stages of the Investiture Controversy. But discontent lingered, especially among Roman nobles who had grown accustomed to influencing papal elections—and didn't care much for Paschal's ascetic style and reformist politics.

Enter Maginulf, a Roman cleric who took the name Sylvester IV when elected by this faction in opposition to Paschal. His claim wasn't widely recognized, but it wasn't entirely insignificant either. Sylvester was crowned in the Lateran Basilica and held parts of the city for a brief time.

Backed by imperial sympathizers, he tried to build a base of support beyond Rome, but Paschal II retained the loyalty of most of Europe's bishops—and more importantly, the Normans. Within a few years,

Sylvester was forced to flee the city, and by 1111, he renounced his claim under pressure.

His resignation effectively marked the end of the line for the old-style, empire-backed antipapacy. After Sylvester IV, future antipopes would emerge from doctrinal splits—not imperial politics.

OUTCOME

Sylvester IV surrendered and was allowed to live out his days quietly in monastic retirement. His defeat helped Paschal II consolidate power and close one of the longest-running chapters of open antipapal defiance.

FUN FACT

Unlike many antipopes, Sylvester IV voluntarily gave up his claim—making him one of the few to exit the role without being deposed, imprisoned, or disfigured. He's proof that sometimes the smart move is knowing when to quit. Also, by 1111, everyone was just tired of the whole imperial antipope thing.

GREGORY VIII

Years active: 1118–1121

Rival pope: Callixtus II

Claim to fame: Installed by imperial forces after the death of Gelasius II, Gregory VIII held Rome for a year but was ultimately ousted by both military pressure and waning legitimacy.

When Pope Gelasius II died in exile in 1119, the Church moved quickly to elect a successor. Reformers—led by powerful French and Roman clergy—chose Callixtus II, a nobleman with strong ties to both the papacy and the growing reform movement. But not everyone was on board.

Emperor Henry V, in the midst of a high-stakes power struggle with the Church over investiture rights, had no intention of allowing another reformist pope to take hold. Instead, he backed the election of Maurice Bourdin, the Archbishop of Braga, who took the name Gregory VIII.

Gregory was no outsider. He had previously served as papal legate and had been elevated by Pope Urban II. But his decision to align with imperial interests—and accept installation by force—instantly branded him a rebel in the eyes of the broader Church.

With German troops at his back, Gregory VIII entered Rome and briefly held the Lateran. But his support crumbled quickly. Most of the clergy refused to recognize him, and his excommunication by the legitimate pope sealed his political isolation. In 1121, Norman forces allied with Callixtus II marched on Rome. Gregory was captured and imprisoned in a monastery, where he remained until his death.

OUTCOME

Gregory VIII was formally anathematized and is universally regarded as an antipope. His reign highlighted the waning effectiveness of imperial-backed antipopes in the post-reform era.

FUN FACT

Gregory's capture marked one of the last instances of a fully armed, German-backed antipope attempting to claim Rome by brute force. After him, antipopes would rely more on internal factionalism than military occupation. Also, going from papal legate to imprisoned antipope is quite the career trajectory.

ANACLETUS II

Years active: 1130–1138

Rival pope: Innocent II

Claim to fame: One of the most significant and controversial antipopes in Church history—held Rome for eight years with majority cardinal support, created the Kingdom of Sicily, and sparked a schism that divided Europe.

If there's one antipope who deserves the label "almost legitimate," it's Anacletus II. Born Pietro Pierleoni to one of Rome's wealthiest and most powerful families, he was a Cluniac monk, a respected cardinal, and a man with impeccable credentials. His great-great-grandfather, a Jewish banker named Baruch (later Benedict after conversion), had made the family fortune, and by 1130, the Pierleoni were one of the dominant forces in Roman politics.

When Pope Honorius II died in February 1130, chaos erupted. A small committee of eight cardinals, led by the papal chancellor Haimeric, rushed through a hasty election and chose Gregorio Papareschi as Pope Innocent II. Hours later, a larger group of cardinals—reportedly the majority—met formally and elected Pietro Pierleoni, who took the name Anacletus II.

Both were consecrated on February 23. Both claimed the papacy. Europe was plunged into schism.

Anacletus had several advantages. He controlled Rome and held the support of most of its clergy and people. The powerful Frangipani family backed him. Most importantly, he had the majority of cardinals on his side—a strong canonical claim. Innocent, meanwhile, was forced to flee to France.

But Innocent had something Anacletus didn't: the support of the great reformers. Bernard of Clairvaux, the most influential churchman in Europe, threw his weight behind Innocent. So did Peter the Venerable of Cluny and Norbert of Xanten. Bernard's rhetoric was vicious—he attacked Anacletus's Jewish ancestry and painted him as illegitimate, despite the electoral irregularities on both sides.

For eight years, Anacletus ruled Rome like a real pope. He appointed bishops, issued decrees, and in 1130 made a decision that would last centuries: he crowned Roger II as King of Sicily, creating a powerful kingdom that unified southern Italy under Norman rule. The Kingdom of Sicily would endure until 1860.

Anacletus had the backing of Scotland, Aquitaine, and parts of northern Italy. But gradually, European monarchs aligned with Innocent. The Holy Roman Emperor Lothair III marched into Italy in 1132 and 1136-37, supporting Innocent militarily. By 1138, Anacletus was isolated but unbowed.

Then he died—still claiming the papacy, still holding Rome, still convinced he was the legitimate successor of Peter.

OUTCOME

After Anacletus's death, his supporters briefly elected Victor IV (Gregorio Conti) as successor, but he submitted to Innocent within a month. Innocent II returned to Rome, convened the Second Lateran

Council in 1139, and systematically erased Anacletus's legacy. His acts were annulled, his appointments reversed, his memory condemned.

But history isn't quite so simple. Modern scholars debate who had the better claim. Anacletus was elected by more cardinals. Innocent's election was rushed and secretive. The schism wasn't about theology—it was about power, politics, and prejudice.

FUN FACT

Anacletus II is sometimes called "the Jewish Pope" because of his ancestry, a label used against him by Bernard of Clairvaux. Voltaire later used the term ironically. Despite being branded an antipope, Anacletus's creation of the Kingdom of Sicily was never reversed—making him possibly the only antipope whose major political act outlasted the Church's condemnation by seven centuries. Also, dying while still in power and still claiming legitimacy makes him one of the most defiant antipopes in history.

VICTOR IV (GREGORIO CONTI)

Year active: 1138

Rival pope: Innocent II

Claim to fame: The brief successor to Anacletus II who surrendered within a month.

When Anacletus II died in January 1138, still claiming the papacy, his supporters weren't quite ready to give up. In a last-ditch effort to continue the schism, they quickly elected Gregorio Conti, a Roman cardinal from the same faction, who took the name Victor IV.

But the situation was hopeless. Anacletus's death had already broken the back of the resistance. Without their charismatic leader, without the Pierleoni family's full backing, and without any realistic path to European recognition, Victor's position collapsed almost immediately.

Innocent II, sensing weakness, moved swiftly. Rather than crush Victor militarily, he offered terms: submit now, and face no punishment. Victor, reading the room, took the deal.

Within a month—possibly within weeks—Victor IV renounced his claim and submitted to Innocent II. In an act of remarkable clemency,

Innocent allowed him to retain his position as cardinal and even gave him the abbacy of a monastery. Victor lived out his days in quiet retirement, never challenging papal authority again.

OUTCOME

Victor IV's rapid surrender marked the definitive end of the Anacletan schism. The Second Lateran Council, convened by Innocent II in 1139, formally condemned Anacletus's legacy and confirmed Innocent's legitimacy.

FUN FACT

Victor IV is one of the rare antipopes who surrendered voluntarily and lived comfortably afterward. His smart exit strategy stands in stark contrast to the fates of most failed papal claimants. Also, the name "Victor IV" would be used again by another antipope just 21 years later, causing centuries of numbering confusion. Medieval record-keeping at its finest.

VICTOR IV (OCTAVIAN)

Years active: 1159–1164

Rival pope: Alexander III

Claim to fame: Elected by a pro-imperial minority after a split conclave, Victor IV triggered one of the longest and most complex schisms of the medieval papacy.

In 1159, the College of Cardinals faced a crisis of consensus. Following the death of Pope Adrian IV, a majority elected Roland of Siena, who took the name Alexander III. But a powerful minority—aligned with Emperor Frederick Barbarossa—objected. Instead, they held their own election and chose Octaviano de Monticelli, who styled himself Victor IV.

This was no small dispute. Victor IV was an experienced diplomat, and with the emperor's backing, he had substantial political muscle. He was consecrated in St. Peter's and controlled Rome for extended periods, depending on who held the city militarily. Several European monarchs—initially including England and parts of the Holy Roman Empire—recognized him.

Meanwhile, Alexander III fled to France and operated in exile, gradually building a base of international support. Over the next five years, the Church was split between two popes, each with their own curia, cardinals, and policies.

Victor IV's reign ended with his death in 1164, but the schism continued. His supporters promptly elected another antipope (Paschal III), extending the crisis for nearly two decades.

OUTCOME

Victor IV's antipapacy helped crystallize the division between imperial loyalty and Church reform, paving the way for broader political conflict across Europe. While ultimately defeated, he posed one of the most credible and sustained threats to the papal office in the 12th century.

FUN FACT

Victor IV's reign coincided with one of the most sophisticated periods of papal diplomacy. Alexander III responded not just with condemnations—but with councils, letters, and shrewd alliances, laying the groundwork for modern Vatican politics. Also, having two popes named Victor IV within 21 years is peak medieval confusion.

PASCHAL III

Years active: 1164–1168

Rival pope: Alexander III

Claim to fame: Successor to Victor IV and architect of the imperial-backed coronation of Emperor Frederick Barbarossa.

If Victor IV represented imperial resistance to the post-reform Church, Paschal III doubled down. Elected by the same faction that had supported Victor, Paschal (born Guido di Crema) was installed in 1164 as a direct continuation of the antipope line. His candidacy was once again backed by Frederick Barbarossa, who was determined to maintain an alternative papacy that would affirm his authority over Church appointments.

Paschal's most notorious act came in 1167, when he crowned Barbarossa Holy Roman Emperor in a grand Roman ceremony—an event meant to echo Charlemagne's coronation and rival Alexander III's authority. The act was purely symbolic: most of Europe did not recognize the coronation, and the ceremony did little to change the balance of power.

Paschal held Rome for brief periods, largely dependent on the shifting presence of imperial troops. His curia was thin, his support fragmented, and his ability to govern limited. Alexander III, operating largely from exile, continued to issue decrees and was increasingly recognized as the true pope by major kingdoms and Church leaders.

Paschal died in 1168, still claiming the title. Like his predecessor, he was succeeded by another antipope (Callixtus III), but the movement was clearly weakening.

OUTCOME

Paschal III's papacy was more ceremonial than functional. Though he played a role in the symbolic politics of the 12th-century schism, he failed to gain substantial traction. His acts—including the canonization of Charlemagne—were later annulled by the Church.

FUN FACT

Paschal III canonized Charlemagne in an attempt to legitimize the imperial cause and align himself with a saintly legacy. The canonization was never recognized by the legitimate Church—and remains one of the most peculiar footnotes in papal history. Charlemagne's sainthood remains disputed to this day in some quarters, all thanks to an antipope's political stunt.

CALLIXTUS III

Years active: 1168–1178

Rival pope: Alexander III

Claim to fame: The final antipope of the imperial-backed line opposing Alexander III during the long papal schism of the 12th century.

When Paschal III died in 1168, the imperial faction supporting antipopes wasn't ready to quit. Their next candidate was John of Struma, who took the name Callixtus III. A Cistercian abbot and imperial loyalist, Callixtus was seen as a compromise figure—someone with clerical respectability who might still carry the torch for Emperor Frederick Barbarossa's efforts to control the papacy.

But by this point, the energy had gone out of the movement. Alexander III had gained solid international support, and the novelty of an imperial antipope had worn thin. Still, Callixtus persisted. For nearly a decade, he issued bulls, consecrated bishops, and maintained a shadow court—though with dwindling influence and very little access to Rome itself.

Eventually, even Barbarossa recognized the futility of the campaign. In 1177, he agreed to negotiate with Alexander III. The following year, a formal reconciliation was reached at the Treaty of Venice. As part of the deal, Callixtus III was asked—gently but firmly—to step aside.

To his credit, he did. Callixtus renounced his claim and submitted to Alexander III, who, in a rare gesture of clemency, appointed him governor of Benevento—a dignified retirement rather than imprisonment or disgrace.

OUTCOME

Callixtus III was the last major antipope of the 12th-century schism. His peaceful surrender marked the final act of the long and bitter standoff between imperial antipopes and Gregorian reformers.

FUN FACT

Because of his orderly retirement and quiet final years, Callixtus III has sometimes been excluded from antipope lists altogether—a curious twist, given he outlasted both Victor IV and Paschal III in office. Also, his name would later be taken by a legitimate pope (Callixtus III, 1455-1458), adding yet another layer of historical confusion. The real Callixtus III is best known for *allegedly* excommunicating Halley's Comet. (This persistent myth was debunked by Vatican archival research—but he did order prayers during the comet's 1456 appearance.)

INNOCENT III

Years active: 1179–1180

Rival pope: Alexander III

Claim to fame: A brief, half-hearted resurgence of antipapacy by hardliners after the Treaty of Venice.

With the long-standing schism finally cooling off, most of Europe had reconciled itself to Alexander III as the legitimate pope. But in 1179, a small faction of hardliners—unwilling to abandon the cause—attempted to restart the schism. They elected Lando di Sezze, a Roman noble, who took the name Innocent III (no relation to the later, far more powerful pope of the same name).

Lando's election was not widely recognized, even within Rome. He never controlled the Lateran, never had significant clerical backing, and never held any meaningful territory. Most historians agree his "papacy" was more symbolic defiance than serious rival governance.

Alexander III, by this point deeply entrenched and diplomatically savvy, wasted little energy on the matter. Innocent III was captured in 1180 and imprisoned in the monastery of La Cava, where he disappears from the historical record.

His brief papacy represents the final sputter of the imperial-aligned faction. After 1180, the great 12th-century schism was truly over.

OUTCOME

Innocent III's brief reign represents a final sputter of resistance from the imperial-aligned factions. After his fall, the schism truly ended. No more imperial antipopes would emerge for over a century.

FUN FACT

The real Pope Innocent III—elected in 1198—was one of the most powerful pontiffs in history. He crowned emperors, launched the Fourth Crusade, and established papal supremacy in European politics. The contrast between the two Innocents is stark: one crowned emperors and launched crusades; the other barely lasted a year and died in a monastery cell. History was not kind to Antipope Innocent III's legacy.

NICHOLAS V

Years active: 1328–1330

Rival pope: John XXII

Claim to fame: Installed by Emperor Louis IV during a showdown with the Avignon papacy, Nicholas was the last serious imperial antipope before the Western Schism.

The 14th century brought a new kind of papal controversy: one centered not in Rome, but in Avignon, France, where the papacy had relocated under French influence. Pope John XXII, residing in Avignon, clashed repeatedly with secular rulers—especially Louis IV of Bavaria, who challenged his legitimacy and claimed the right to appoint bishops and influence papal elections.

In 1328, Louis IV marched into Rome with his army and declared John XXII deposed. In his place, he installed Pietro Rainalducci, a Franciscan friar and theological opponent of John, who took the name Nicholas V.

Nicholas was crowned in St. Peter's with all the traditional ceremony —but little recognition outside of imperial circles. Even within the Empire, his authority was debated. While Louis IV wanted a pope who would legitimize his reign, few believed Nicholas had the stature to rally the Church around him.

Nicholas spent about two years holding court in Rome, issuing proclamations and attempting to fill Church offices. But when imperial support waned, so did his papacy. In 1330, he submitted to John XXII, publicly repenting and seeking forgiveness. The Avignon pope accepted his surrender—but didn't let him off the hook. Nicholas was imprisoned in Avignon for the rest of his life.

OUTCOME

Nicholas V was the last imperial-backed antipope before the Western Schism. His career revealed how fragile papal legitimacy had become—and how little appetite remained for emperors trying to install their own pontiffs.

FUN FACT

Despite being publicly humiliated and imprisoned for life, Nicholas V was treated with relative dignity in Avignon. Some accounts suggest he lived comfortably and even acted as an informal advisor—just no longer as pope. Also, he's the last antipope whose primary claim came from imperial backing rather than internal Church politics. After Nicholas, antipopes would emerge from schisms within the Church itself.

Part Four

THE SCHISMATICS

(14th–15th centuries)

If earlier antipopes were rebels or imperial pawns, the Western Schism created rival papacies that were fully institutionalized. These weren't lone claimants—they were men elected by cardinals, backed by monarchs, and treated by millions as the true successors of Peter.

It began in 1378 with the election of Urban VI, an Italian pope whose erratic behavior led many cardinals to declare the election invalid. Their response? Elect Clement VII, who set up court in Avignon. Thus began a decades-long split where two (and at one point three) men claimed to be pope simultaneously.

Entire kingdoms aligned themselves along schismatic lines. There were two sets of cardinals, two papal courts, two lines of succession. Councils were held to fix the problem—and only made it worse. The Church excommunicated itself repeatedly. It was an era of deep institutional embarrassment and global confusion.

These antipopes weren't fringe—they were half the Church. And their reigns were long, consequential, and, in many cases, ended only after their deaths. This is the climax of papal disunity—the moment when the papacy fractured not at the edges, but at the center.

CLEMENT VII

Years active: 1378–1394

Rival pope: Urban VI

Claim to fame: The first antipope of the Western Schism, Clement was elected by cardinals who claimed the Roman pope had been chosen under duress—sparking nearly 40 years of divided papal rule.

When Pope Gregory XI died in 1378, the papacy had only just returned to Rome from its long exile in Avignon. The Roman public, weary of foreign popes, rioted to demand an Italian successor. Under heavy pressure—with mobs surrounding the conclave shouting threats—the cardinals elected Bartolomeo Prignano, who became Urban VI.

It didn't go well.

Urban's fiery temper and harsh reforms quickly alienated the very cardinals who had elected him. Just months later, those cardinals regrouped, declared Urban's election invalid—arguing it had been made under mob intimidation—and elected one of their own: Robert of Geneva, who took the name Clement VII.

Now the Church had two popes: Urban in Rome, and Clement in Avignon. And not just popes-in-name—each had a college of cardinals, issued decrees, appointed bishops, and commanded allegiance from entire nations. France, Scotland, Castile, and Aragon backed Clement. England, the Holy Roman Empire, and most of northern Italy supported Urban.

Clement styled himself the true pope, leaning heavily on French political support. But without Rome or universal backing, his position was shaky. He spent most of his reign in Avignon, consolidating his administration and defending his legitimacy in a flurry of letters, theological arguments, and diplomatic overtures.

The schism divided not just nations but religious orders, universities, and even individual dioceses. Saints supported opposing sides. Theologians wrote treatises proving their pope was legitimate. It was ecclesiastical civil war.

OUTCOME

Clement VII died in 1394, never having set foot in Rome. But the damage was done. His papacy entrenched the Avignon line of antipopes, institutionalizing the split and making eventual reconciliation far harder.

FUN FACT

Before becoming antipope, Clement (Robert of Geneva) led the brutal suppression of a rebellion in Cesena, where thousands were killed. The incident earned him the nickname "Butcher of Cesena"—not exactly the image most popes aim for. Also, having "Butcher of Cesena" on your résumé probably didn't help convince people you were the legitimate vicar of Christ.

BENEDICT XIII

Years active: 1394–1423

Rival popes: Boniface IX, Innocent VII, Gregory XII, and later Martin V

Claim to fame: The most stubborn antipope in Church history—refusing to step down even after all his allies deserted him.

When Clement VII died, the Avignon cardinals hoped for unity. Instead, they got Pedro de Luna, a brilliant but intransigent canon lawyer who became Benedict XIII. At first, his election looked like a strategic move. Benedict was respected, diplomatic, and seemed open to resolving the schism.

That... did not happen.

Efforts to unite the Church repeatedly fell apart. Negotiations with the Roman line stalled. The French king, initially Benedict's key supporter, withdrew recognition in 1398, effectively declaring the papal throne vacant. Benedict held out anyway, even as one kingdom after another abandoned him.

By 1409, the Council of Pisa tried to solve the problem by deposing both reigning popes and electing a third—Alexander V. But Benedict refused to step down. So did the Roman pope, Gregory XII. Now, for the first time, the Church had three rival popes, each with their own court.

Benedict's refusal to compromise became legendary. He eventually fled to the fortress of Peñíscola, on the coast of modern-day Spain, where he held court for over a decade with just a handful of loyal cardinals. Even after the Council of Constance resolved the schism in 1417 by electing Martin V, Benedict refused to recognize it.

He died in 1423, still claiming to be pope, at approximately age 95. To the very end, he insisted he was the legitimate successor of Peter.

OUTCOME

Benedict XIII's reign extended well beyond the end of the Western Schism—by sheer force of will. His refusal to abdicate helped delay Church unity for years and inspired some truly impressive levels of stubbornness.

FUN FACT

At the time of his death, Benedict's "papal court" had shrunk to just one cardinal—Jean Carrier. That cardinal then elected his own pope—Clement VIII—sparking a tiny, two-man schism that limped into the 1430s before fizzling out. Benedict XIII: so stubborn that even his death couldn't end his schism.

ALEXANDER V

Years active: 1409–1410

Rival popes: Gregory XII and Benedict XIII

Claim to fame: Elected to heal the schism... and accidentally made it worse.

By 1409, the situation was dire. Europe was divided between two popes—Gregory XII in Rome and Benedict XIII in Avignon—neither willing to resign. In response, a group of cardinals from both camps convened the Council of Pisa, hoping to sidestep both claimants and elect a unifying figure.

Enter Petros Philargos, a respected Franciscan theologian and Archbishop of Milan. Known for his piety and learning, he was elected as Alexander V—a compromise candidate meant to restore order.

But instead of ending the schism, Alexander's election escalated it. Neither Gregory nor Benedict accepted the council's authority. So instead of one pope, or two, the Church now had three.

Alexander operated from Pisa and later Bologna, garnering support from parts of Italy, France, and England. He made sweeping promises of reform, particularly to religious orders and universities, and distributed papal benefices generously. But his actual reforms were few, and his authority was contested everywhere.

He died suddenly in 1410—possibly of illness, possibly poisoned by his successor, Baldassare Cossa (who became John XXIII). His death came too quickly for him to make any real impact.

OUTCOME

Alexander V's election was well-intentioned but disastrous. His papacy failed to unite the Church and inadvertently deepened the crisis. He is now considered an antipope, since the Pisan line was not validated by the Church after the schism ended.

FUN FACT

The next real Pope Alexander—Alexander VI (the Borgia pope)—refused to count Alexander V as legitimate. That's why Alexander VI kept the number VI, not VII. Even the corrupt popes respected papal math. Also, dying within a year of being elected "to fix everything" is a particularly tragic form of historical irony.

JOHN XXIII

Years active: 1410–1415

Rival popes: Gregory XII, Benedict XIII, later Martin V

Claim to fame: The final Pisan-line antipope—colorful, controversial, and eventually reconciled after the Council of Constance.

When Alexander V died in 1410, the cardinals who had supported the Council of Pisa wasted no time electing a successor: Baldassare Cossa, a Neapolitan cardinal and skilled administrator with a reputation for cunning diplomacy—and moral flexibility. He took the name John XXIII, determined to press forward with the effort to unify the Church.

Cossa was no idealist. His papacy was marked by lavish spending, political intrigue, and military alliances. He raised armies, launched aggressive tax campaigns, and operated more like a Renaissance prince than a spiritual leader. Still, he commanded real influence—especially in northern Italy and parts of the Holy Roman Empire.

But like his predecessor, John XXIII couldn't resolve the schism. By 1413, the Church still had three popes: Gregory XII (Rome), Benedict XIII (Avignon), and John XXIII (Pisa). None would resign.

With pressure mounting, Holy Roman Emperor Sigismund called the Council of Constance (1414–1418). John agreed to participate, hoping to direct the proceedings in his favor. Instead, he was deposed. Charges were brought against him—including simony, fornication, and murder (though many were likely exaggerated or politically motivated). He fled the council in disguise, was captured, and imprisoned.

In 1415, Gregory XII voluntarily resigned. In 1417, the council elected Martin V, ending the schism. A few years later, John XXIII submitted to Martin and was forgiven. Martin elevated him to Cardinal Bishop of Frascati, allowing him to end his days in Rome with some dignity.

OUTCOME

Though once seen as an antipope, John XXIII's legacy became ambiguous after his reconciliation. His tomb, designed by Donatello, still stands in Florence's Baptistery—a remarkable honor for a deposed papal claimant.

FUN FACT

Because this John XXIII was retroactively deemed an antipope, the next pope named John—elected in 1958—chose to take the name John XXIII anyway, effectively restarting the numbering from the last valid John. It's one of the few times a papal number was officially recycled. Also, John XXIII (the antipope) is one of the few failed popes to get a tomb by a world-famous Renaissance sculptor. Not a bad consolation prize.

CLEMENT VIII

Years active: 1423–1429

Rival pope: Martin V

Claim to fame: Elected by the last remaining cardinal from Benedict XIII's court—extending the Avignon schism long after everyone else had gone home.

Even after the Council of Constance declared unity restored and crowned Martin V as pope in 1417, Benedict XIII—the last Avignon antipope—refused to accept it. He died in 1423, still claiming the papacy. And astonishingly, his one remaining cardinal elected a successor: Gil Sánchez Muñoz y Carbón, who became Clement VIII.

Clement was the head of what was essentially a two-man Vatican, holed up in the fortress of Peñíscola. His jurisdiction extended across the castle grounds and possibly a few confused households in Aragon.

Despite the absurdity of his claim, Clement operated like a proper pope. He issued bulls, corresponded with monarchs, and maintained the ceremonial dignity of the office. For a while, the king of Aragon even supported him—until the political cost outweighed the novelty.

By 1429, Clement stepped down voluntarily. In a rare moment of tidy closure, he reconciled with Pope Martin V, was rewarded with the bishopric of Majorca, and faded from history without drama.

OUTCOME

Clement VIII marked the final flicker of the Western Schism. After his resignation, no serious papal rivalries persisted for centuries—at least not ones backed by cardinals and kingdoms.

FUN FACT

Because Clement VIII was elected by only one cardinal, some historians call him the "antipope with the smallest conclave in history." There were more people present at his coronation than at his election. Also, getting to retire as a bishop after being an antipope is an unusually good deal—most antipopes ended up in prison or worse.

BENEDICT XIV (BERNARD GARNIER)

Years active: 1424–c. 1430

Rival pope: Martin V

Claim to fame: The "Hidden Pope" elected in secret to continue Benedict XIII's line—operated entirely in hiding and may be the only pope to rule from a cave.

When Benedict XIII died in 1423, most of Europe had moved on from the Western Schism. But not Jean Carrier—a die-hard cardinal from Rodez who refused to accept unity. He considered the newly elected Martin V a usurper and resolved to keep the Avignon line alive. Unfortunately, there weren't many schism supporters left. So, Carrier appointed himself the College of Cardinals and secretly "elected" Bernard Garnier as pope.

A local chaplain with no power base of his own, Garnier took the name Benedict XIV and went into deep hiding—allegedly living in caves, barns, and remote safehouses throughout southern France. His papacy had no court, no curia, and barely a congregation. Still, he continued to act as if he held real papal authority, writing letters and occasionally receiving clandestine visitors.

The Church barely acknowledged his existence, and even most of Benedict XIII's former supporters ignored him. His entire "reign" was essentially a political hallucination kept alive by one man's stubbornness and another's willingness to play along.

Garnier died around 1430, still in hiding. His papacy left no mark—except as one of the strangest footnotes of the Schism. But incredibly, it didn't end there.

OUTCOME

Garnier's death in hiding closed one chapter, but Jean Carrier wasn't done yet. After Garnier died, Carrier would elect himself pope—making him the only person to be both the entire College of Cardinals and the pope simultaneously.

FUN FACT

Benedict XIV is sometimes referred to as the "underground pope," not for any radical theology—but because he may have literally governed from a hole in the ground. His cave-dwelling papacy makes him possibly the most literal "underground" religious movement leader in Christian history. Also, "pope in a cave" sounds like the setup to a very strange medieval folktale.

BENEDICT XIV (JEAN CARRIER)

Years active: 1430–c. 1437

Rival pope: Eugene IV

Claim to fame: The only known one-man conclave to elect two antipopes—including himself.

Jean Carrier had been a trusted follower of Benedict XIII and had singlehandedly elected Bernard Garnier to keep the Avignon line alive. But when Garnier died around 1430, the "conclave" was once again reduced to just one man: Carrier himself.

Undeterred, he declared himself pope and retained the name Benedict XIV, making him the only person in history to be both the College of Cardinals and the pope in one body. He had no supporters, no territories, and no credibility—but in his mind, he was the last true pontiff of Benedict XIII's line.

Carrier continued to operate from the shadows, issuing occasional proclamations and writing letters to monarchs who never replied. But the charade didn't last. Eventually, he was arrested and imprisoned by authorities loyal to Pope Eugene IV. His papal career ended in a cell, without even a single schismatic follower to defend him.

Carrier died in captivity sometime after 1437. His bizarre self-appointment marked the absolute collapse of the Avignon line. Even other schismatics regarded him as a deluded crank.

OUTCOME

Carrier died in captivity, and with him died the last remnant of the Avignon schism. No one carried the torch forward. The mini-schism was finally, definitively over.

FUN FACT

Carrier was the only antipope in history to declare himself pope twice—once as kingmaker when he elected Garnier, and once as king when he elected himself. His one-man conclave is either the most audacious or most pathetic moment in antipope history, depending on your perspective. Also, electing yourself pope when you're the only cardinal left is technically following Church law—just not the spirit of it.

FELIX V

Years active: 1439–1449

Rival popes: Eugene IV, then Nicholas V

Claim to fame: The last historical antipope, elected by the Council of Basel and supported by a chunk of Europe—briefly.

By the mid-15th century, conciliarism—the idea that Church councils held authority over popes—was at its peak. The Council of Basel, increasingly hostile to Pope Eugene IV, declared him deposed in 1439 and elected its own pope: Amadeus VIII, Duke of Savoy, who took the name Felix V.

Unlike the ragtag claimants who came before him, Felix had real political muscle. He was wealthy, respected, and ruled a significant territory. His election was supported by parts of the Holy Roman Empire, Switzerland, and some French clergy. For a moment, the schism seemed dangerously revived.

But support for Felix never became widespread. The theological tide was turning back toward papal supremacy, and the council's authority eroded. After Eugene IV died in 1447, Nicholas V was elected with broad backing, and most of Europe fell in line.

Felix saw the writing on the wall. In 1449, he resigned—a rare, graceful exit for an antipope. He reconciled with Nicholas V and returned to secular life in Savoy, where he remained active in politics and died peacefully in 1451.

OUTCOME

Felix V is considered the last official antipope recognized by Church historians. His resignation helped bring the age of papal rivalries to a quiet, diplomatic close.

FUN FACT

Felix V's tomb in Hautecombe Abbey still refers to him as pontifex maximus—a final wink to a decade-long papal adventure. He's also the only antipope who was a ruling duke at the time of his election, making him possibly the wealthiest antipope in history. Retiring from the papacy to go back to being a duke is quite the fallback plan.

Part Five

THE POST-SCHISM FRINGE

(16th century to present)

Once the dust of the Western Schism settled and the papacy returned to relative normalcy, the antipopes didn't go away. They just got weirder.

No longer crowned by kings or surrounded by cardinals, modern antipopes tend to emerge from the outer edges of Catholicism. They arise in times of tension—often in response to Vatican II, perceived modernism, or geopolitical change—and appoint themselves as papal counterweights. Their conclaves are small (sometimes one person), their reach limited, and their headgear occasionally homemade.

From Spanish mystics to Kansas farmers to visionary Frenchmen, this final group of antipopes claims the same spiritual authority—but without the armies, basilicas, or incense. Some create full churches with new liturgies and hierarchies. Others remain mostly symbolic.

They're not just anomalies—they're a reminder that papal authority is as much a matter of perception as tradition. And that the idea of "pope" still has cultural weight—even without St. Peter's Square.

CLEMENT XV (MICHEL COLLIN)

Years active: 1950–1974

Real name: Michel Collin (later styled: Michel I)

Claim to fame: Claimed he was secretly appointed pope by Christ himself after Pius XII failed to defend the world against communism.

Long before Pope Michael or the Palmarian movement, there was Michel Collin, a French priest who declared himself pope in 1950, styling himself Clement XV. The mid-20th century was full of anxiety—war, communism, Church reform—and Collin was convinced that Pope Pius XII had failed his divine mandate.

So, Collin claimed that Jesus Christ personally appeared to him and made him pope. No conclave, no votes, no fanfare—just divine appointment.

Collin founded a small sect known as the Apostles of Infinite Love, which mixed Catholic teachings with apocalyptic warnings, mystical revelations, and heavy Marian devotion. His papacy included bizarre doctrinal declarations and private visions of heavenly councils. His writings were prolific and often deeply esoteric.

While his following remained small, he ordained bishops, issued encyclicals, and maintained that he was the only valid pontiff for over two decades. He died in 1974, still claiming the papal throne.

OUTCOME

Collin's papacy was part of a broader wave of ultra-traditionalist splinter groups responding to modernity and the perceived liberalization of the Church. His movement continued after his death, electing new "popes" and evolving into one of the more organized modern antipope movements.

FUN FACT

After Collin's death, his sect continued—electing new "popes" and canonizing Clement XV as a saint. Some offshoots of his movement still exist in Canada and France, often with minimal online presence and maximal secrecy. Also, claiming Jesus personally appointed you pope is a bold move that's very hard to fact-check.

GREGORY XVII (CLEMENTE DOMÍNGUEZ Y GÓMEZ)

Years active: 1978–2005

Real name: Clemente Domínguez y Gómez

Claim to fame: Claimed to receive visions of Christ and the Virgin Mary—then declared himself pope after Paul VI's death, creating the Palmarian Catholic Church.

The Palmarian Catholic Church, based in El Palmar de Troya, Spain, is one of the most organized and theatrical breakaway papacies in history. At its center was Clemente Domínguez y Gómez, a Spanish mystic who began receiving alleged visions of Jesus and Mary in the late 1960s.

Over time, Clemente's visions became increasingly political. By the mid-1970s, he declared that Pope Paul VI had been replaced by an impostor, the Vatican had fallen to Satan, and that the true papacy had been transferred—quietly—to Spain.

In 1978, after Paul VI's death, Clemente declared himself pope, taking the name Gregory XVII. He donned ornate robes, built a massive Palmarian basilica, and created his own cardinals, many of whom were his closest friends. His papacy was intensely secretive, apocalyptic, and heavy on moral purity—though Gregory himself was later accused of serious financial and sexual misconduct.

He died in 2005 and was succeeded by a line of Palmarian popes, including Peter II, who later defected, denounced the sect, and published a tell-all memoir exposing the movement's inner workings.

OUTCOME

Gregory XVII's claim created a full-blown parallel Church, complete with its own feast days, saints, and even a "revised Bible." The Palmarian movement survives today, though in diminished form, with a small community still maintaining the basilica in Spain.

FUN FACT

At its height, the Palmarian Church claimed to have excommunicated the entire population of the planet, save for its own members. That's one way to keep the doctrine pure. Also, Gregory XVII canonized Francisco Franco (the Spanish dictator) and Christopher Columbus, which tells you a lot about the Palmarian Church's political leanings.

POPE MICHAEL (DAVID BAWDEN)

Years active: 1990–2022

Real name: David Bawden

Claim to fame: Elected pope by a conclave of six people—including his parents—in the Bawden family's thrift store in Kansas.

In the summer of 1990, six sedevacantist Catholics gathered in Belvue, Kansas, to solve what they believed was the biggest crisis in modern Catholicism: there had been no valid pope since 1958. So, naturally, they held a conclave.

They elected David Bawden, a former seminarian and long-time critic of the post-Vatican II Church. He took the name Pope Michael, claiming to be the one true successor of Peter. His papacy, headquartered in a modest rural home, included no Swiss Guard, no Vatican bureaucracy, and—initially—no bishops. But it did have a website.

Pope Michael took his role seriously. He ordained himself a bishop in 2011 (with the help of a sympathetic Brazilian bishop who later withdrew his support) and continued to publish theological works, online catechisms, and papal declarations—all from rural Kansas. He gained a modest following in traditionalist circles, especially online, and became a minor Catholic internet personality.

He engaged with critics, gave interviews, appeared in documentaries, and maintained a YouTube presence. He was earnest, devout, and utterly convinced of his legitimacy. Though widely regarded as a fringe figure, Pope Michael commanded genuine respect from some corners of the sedevacantist movement.

He died in July 2022, having served as "pope" for 32 years—longer than many legitimate popes.

OUTCOME

The original "YouTube Pope," Pope Michael led perhaps the most earnest papal claim in modern memory—equal parts sincere, eccentric, and baffling. After his death, his small community debated whether to hold another conclave, though as of 2024, no official successor has been named.

FUN FACT

Pope Michael's election conclave included his parents, which has to be one of the most wholesome origin stories for an antipope. Also, he's one of the few antipopes to actively engage with the internet, doing AMAs (Ask Me Anything sessions), interviews, and even appearing in a Vice documentary. His digital footprint is larger than most medieval popes.

Part Three

WARS OF THE TIARA

Where power meets piety... and explodes in a puff of incense.

This section isn't just a parade of names—it's the highlight reel of papal chaos. The major schisms, the wildest depositions, and the emperors who just couldn't mind their business. If the earlier chapters showed us who the antipopes were, this is where we dig into why it kept happening—and how messy it got when sacred office met secular ambition.

THE GREAT PAPAL SCHISMS, RANKED BY DYSFUNCTION

THE WESTERN SCHISM (1378–1417): THE TRIPLE POPE DISASTER

The crown jewel of papal dysfunction. It began when Urban VI was elected—but was so unpleasant that many cardinals fled and elected Clement VII instead.

Boom: two popes.

Then a council was held to fix the problem—and elected a third pope (Alexander V, followed by John XXIII). For nearly 40 years, Europe had multiple popes, dueling excommunications, and a theological migraine no one could cure.

Each pope had his own court, his own cardinals, and his own line of succession. France backed Avignon. England backed Rome. Scotland backed whoever France backed just to annoy England. Religious orders split down the middle. Universities declared allegiance. Saints ended up on opposing sides.

Winner: Nobody. Everyone lost credibility.

Resolution: The Council of Constance finally convinced (or forced) all popes to resign—except Benedict XIII, who held out in a Spanish fortress until his death in 1423, still claiming to be pope. Martin V was elected in 1417, ending the main schism, though Benedict's stubborn mini-schism continued.

THE ANACLETAN SCHISM (1130–1138): THE EIGHT-YEAR ROMAN STANDOFF

When Pope Honorius II died in 1130, two rival elections happened on the same day. A small group of cardinals rushed through a hasty election of Innocent II. Hours later, a larger group—reportedly the majority—formally elected Pietro Pierleoni as Anacletus II.

Both were consecrated on February 23. Europe was divided.

What made this schism particularly significant: Anacletus held Rome for eight years, had majority cardinal support, and created the Kingdom of Sicily—a political unit that would last until 1860. He wasn't some fringe claimant; he was a serious rival with legitimate backing.

But he faced vicious opposition. Bernard of Clairvaux attacked his Jewish ancestry and rallied European monarchs against him. Gradually, support shifted to Innocent II, backed by the Holy Roman Emperor and Norman forces.

Anacletus died in 1138, still in power in Rome, still claiming legitimacy. His successor, Victor IV (Gregorio Conti), submitted to Innocent within a month, ending the schism.

Legacy: A gilded reminder that canonical elections meant little when politics and prejudice were in play. Also, one of the few schisms where the antipope arguably had the better electoral claim.

Fun Fact: The Kingdom of Sicily, created by antipope Anacletus II, outlasted his condemnation by seven centuries—making it possibly the most durable legacy of any antipope in history.

THE AVIGNON PAPACY (1309–1377): THE BABYLONIAN CAPTIVITY OF THE PAPACY

For nearly 70 years, the popes lived not in Rome, but in a luxury papal palace in Avignon, France. Technically legitimate, but politically suspect—the Avignon popes were seen as puppets of the French crown. The real crisis came after they returned to Rome, died, and triggered the Western Schism.

Legacy: A gilded cage for the papacy, setting the stage for the double-papacy disaster. Also, proof that even legitimate popes can lose credibility when they're too cozy with secular power.

Fun Fact: The Avignon popes may have had the best wine cellars in Church history. The Palace of the Popes in Avignon is still standing and remains one of the largest Gothic structures in Europe—a monument to papal wealth and French influence.

DOUBLE ELECTIONS (498, 530, 687...): PICK A POPE, ANY POPE

Back in the early centuries, Rome had no chill when it came to electing popes. Two factions would declare rival victors and both would claim the tiara. Sometimes the issue was resolved by a mob. Sometimes an emperor weighed in. Sometimes one pope just died faster.

Most common outcome: civil unrest and an antipope with a short reign. These weren't ideological battles—they were power struggles wrapped in theological language.

Notable cases:

- Laurentius vs. Symmachus (498-506): Required a pagan king to referee
- Dioscorus vs. Boniface II (530): Solved by Dioscorus dying after 22 days
- Theodore vs. Paschal vs. Sergius (687): Three-way split that ended in conspiracy charges

THE CONCILIARISM CRISIS: WHEN THE CHURCH TRIED DEMOCRACY

After the chaos of the Western Schism, some theologians said, "What if... the Church ruled itself?"

Thus, conciliarism: the belief that ecumenical councils had more authority than the pope. The idea gained ground fast, especially at the Councils of Pisa, Constance, and Basel—but ran into one big problem: popes don't like being overruled.

The Council of Pisa (1409) tried to solve the two-pope problem by electing a third—making things worse. The Council of Constance (1414-1418) actually succeeded by deposing all claimants and electing Martin V. The Council of Basel (1431-1449) tried again with Felix V, but by then the movement had lost steam.

Eventually, the papacy reasserted supremacy and conciliarism was quietly retired... though not before a few extra popes were added to the mix.

Legacy: A brief moment when it seemed like the Church might embrace collective governance. Spoiler: it didn't stick.

MOST DRAMATIC DEPOSITIONS

POPE BENEDICT IX: THREE-TIME POPE, ZERO-TIME SAINT

Sold the papacy, reclaimed it, and was finally deposed for being too scandalous, even by 11th-century standards. Once described as "a demon from hell in the disguise of a priest." His three separate reigns (1032-1044, 1045, 1047-1048) were marked by simony, violence, and general mayhem. Not technically an antipope himself, but his chaos created antipopes.

COUNCIL OF CONSTANCE (1414–1418): THE PAPAL HUNGER GAMES

Three rival popes walk into a council. Only one walks out.

This council ended the Western Schism by firing all three popes and installing Martin V as the new and only one. It was like ecclesiastical Survivor: alliances, backstabbing, exile, and a surprise victor. John XXIII (antipope) tried to flee in disguise. Gregory XII voluntarily resigned. Benedict XIII refused to acknowledge the council's authority and died in exile still claiming the papacy.

ANTIPOPE CONSTANTINE II: THE FORCEFUL ONE

Seized the papacy by armed force in 767, reigned for about a year... then was blinded, imprisoned, had his tongue cut out, and was paraded through Rome by a rival faction. The medieval Church was not subtle about its disapproval.

ANTIPOPE FELIX II: INSTALLED BY AN ARIAN EMPEROR, FORGOTTEN BY HISTORY

Backed by Emperor Constantius II but ultimately exiled when the legitimate Pope Liberius returned in triumph. Now considered a textbook case of "what not to do" when picking popes. His main achievement was getting his name added to the papal numbering by accident.

EULALIUS (418): BANISHED FOR COMING BACK TOO SOON

After a disputed election, Emperor Honorius told Eulalius to chill outside Rome while things cooled off.

Eulalius defied orders and returned early to celebrate Easter Mass.

Outcome: Instant disqualification. Banished. That's what you get for showing up uninvited to your own papacy. The emperor switched his support to Boniface I, and Eulalius vanished from history.

JOHN XVI: THE MOST BRUTAL END

After being captured in 998, John XVI was tortured, blinded, had his nose, ears, and tongue removed, then paraded through Rome on a donkey facing backward. He survived and lived out his days in a monastery. This exceptionally cruel treatment stood out even in an era known for harsh punishments.

THE EMPEROR PROBLEM

If there was an antipope crisis, there was probably an emperor nearby making things worse.

THE HOLY ROMAN EMPIRE: TOO MANY OPINIONS, NOT ENOUGH THEOLOGY

From Otto I to Henry IV to Frederick Barbarossa, the emperors of the Holy Roman Empire saw the pope as a bishop with perks, not a spiritual sovereign.

They frequently installed their own popes, exiled sitting ones, or dragged the papacy into their wars.

Result? Chaos, schisms, and the Investiture Controversy, which sounds boring but involved bishops being appointed like chess pieces and two decades of Clement III ruling as an imperial puppet.

Notable Imperial Antipopes:

- Felix II (355-365): Installed by Arian-sympathizing Emperor Constantius II
- Clement III (1080-1100): Longest-reigning antipope, backed by Henry IV for 20 years

- Gregory VIII (1118-1121): Last serious armed German-backed antipope attempt
- Nicholas V (1328-1330): Final imperial antipope before the Western Schism

LAY INVESTITURE: WHO GETS TO PICK THE BISHOPS?

For centuries, emperors believed it was their right to "invest" bishops with symbols of power—essentially appointing Church officials like they were government positions.

The Church disagreed—violently.

Multiple antipopes emerged from this feud, including Clement III, who was installed by Emperor Henry IV during his legendary beef with Pope Gregory VII. The controversy lasted from roughly 1050 to 1122 and reshaped the relationship between Church and state.

Resolution: The Concordat of Worms (1122) established that the Church would appoint bishops spiritually, but emperors could still invest them with temporal authority. It was a compromise that satisfied no one but ended the worst of the fighting.

THE BYZANTINE INTERFERENCE

Eastern Roman (Byzantine) emperors frequently meddled in papal elections during the early medieval period, especially in the 6th-8th centuries when parts of Italy were still under Byzantine control.

Examples:

- Felix II was appointed by the Arian-leaning Emperor Constantius II, triggering theological and political uproar
- Paschal (687) conspired with the Byzantine exarch of Ravenna, offering bribes for military backing
- John XVI (997-998) was backed by Byzantine Emperor Basil II as a counterweight to German influence

Outcome: Byzantine meddling gradually decreased as the Eastern and Western Churches drifted apart, culminating in the Great Schism of 1054. After that, Byzantine emperors had their own ecclesiastical problems.

THE AFTERLIVES OF ANTIPOPES

What happens after you lose the keys to the kingdom?

Not all antipopes ended in disgrace. A few were reconciled, forgiven, even canonized. Others disappeared into obscurity or clung to their claim until the bitter end.

THE RECONCILED

Hippolytus: The very first antipope eventually reconciled with the Church and died a martyr. He's even a saint now—feast day August 13, shared with Pope Pontian. Moral? It's never too late for a comeback. Or maybe dying in the mines of Sardinia earns you sainthood regardless of your antipope status.

John XXIII (antipope): Submitted to Martin V after being deposed, was elevated to Cardinal Bishop of Frascati, and got a tomb designed by Donatello. Not a bad retirement plan for a failed pope. His reconciliation with the Church was so complete that some historians debate whether he should even be called an antipope.

Felix V: The last "official" antipope of the Western Schism resigned voluntarily and went back to being the Duke of Savoy. Graceful exit?

Rare, but not impossible. He was later made a cardinal and lived peacefully until his death in 1451.

THE STUBBORN

Benedict XIII: Refused to resign for three decades. Even after everyone left—including St. Vincent Ferrer and the king of Aragon—he held court in a fortress with one cardinal. Died in 1423, still pope in his own head. His one remaining cardinal then elected Clement VIII, extending the mini-schism for another six years.

Anacletus II: Never reconciled. Held Rome for eight years with majority cardinal backing, created the Kingdom of Sicily, and died in power in 1138—still claiming legitimacy, still convinced he was right. His legacy was systematically erased by Innocent II, but modern historians debate whether he had the better claim.

THE FORGOTTEN

Adalbert (1101): So obscure that historians debate whether he existed at all. If he did, he made no impact whatsoever. His papacy—if real—lasted weeks and left no documents, no followers, no legacy. The perfect example of historical erasure.

Philip (768): Proclaimed pope for one day, then returned to his monastery. Smart man. Sometimes the best move is recognizing when you're in over your head.

THE POSTHUMOUS VINDICATION

Callixtus III (not the antipope, but related): He posthumously rehabilitated Joan of Arc. Not all papal politics ends in fire and brimstone. Sometimes centuries later, someone fixes your mistakes.

THE INTERNET AGE

Pope Michael (David Bawden, 1990-2022): Lived as a self-declared pope in Kansas for 32 years, with a few loyal followers and a functioning website. His papacy may be over, but his myth lives on in Catholic internet lore. He engaged with critics, did AMAs, appeared in documentaries, and maintained his claim until his death in 2022.

Some antipopes were forgotten almost instantly. Others linger in odd footnotes, conspiracy theories, or YouTube documentaries with dramatic Gregorian chant intros and 2,000 views.

TIMELINE OF PAPAL DISUNITY

A rough guide to the holy mess.

3rd–5th c.: Early theological rivals like Hippolytus and Novatian challenge orthodoxy and papal authority over penance and purity.

6th–9th c.: Imperial interference leads to puppet antipopes backed by emperors. Byzantine and later Carolingian rulers treat the papacy as another bishopric to control.

10th–11th c.: Medieval chaos = overlapping elections, armed takeovers, and feuding noble families. The Crescentii and Tusculani families turn Rome into a battleground. Reform movements begin pushing back.

11th–12th c.: Investiture Controversy produces long-running imperial antipopes like Clement III (20 years) and triggers fundamental debates about Church-state relations. Victor IV and successors create sustained schism opposing Alexander III.

1130–1138: Anacletan Schism divides Europe between Innocent II and Anacletus II, who creates Kingdom of Sicily and holds Rome with majority cardinal support.

1309–1377: Avignon Papacy puts popes under French thumb. Technically legitimate but politically compromised. Sets stage for Western Schism.

1378–1417: Western Schism splits the papacy two (then three) ways. Clement VII establishes Avignon line. Council of Pisa makes it worse by electing Alexander V. Benedict XIII refuses to quit even after Council of Constance.

1417: Council of Constance ends the Schism (mostly) with election of Martin V.

1423–1437: Mini-schism continues as Benedict XIII's remaining cardinal elects Clement VIII, then Benedict XIV (Garnier), then declares himself Benedict XIV (Carrier). The world's saddest papal succession.

1439–1449: Felix V, elected by Council of Basel, becomes the last historically recognized antipope. Resigns peacefully in 1449.

15th–16th c.: Conciliarist popes and fringe claimants fade out as papal supremacy is reasserted.

20th–21st c.: Post-Vatican II era gives rise to sedevacantist claimants and micro-papacies (Palmarian, Kansas-based, French mystical movements, etc.). No armies or kingdoms, but plenty of websites.

Part Four

TRIVIA, TIMELINES & HOLY CHAOS

Because Church history should come with scoreboards.

This section is the fun part—the rankings, the oddities, and the papal moments that make you say "wait, *what*?" If earlier chapters gave you the history, this is where we crown winners, call out losers, and tally up the most convincing, most ridiculous, and most forgotten players in the antipope game. Think of it as papal March Madness, minus the brackets but with all the chaos.

TOP 5 MOST CONVINCING ANTIPOPES

"Honestly, he had a point..."

1. **Anacletus II (1130–1138)** The most convincing antipope in history. Elected by the majority of cardinals, held Rome for eight years, backed by most of the city's clergy and people, and created the Kingdom of Sicily—a political unit that lasted until 1860. His main disadvantage? Bernard of Clairvaux's vicious propaganda campaign attacking his Jewish ancestry. Modern historians still debate whether he had the better claim than Innocent II.

2. **Hippolytus (c. 217–235)** The OG antipope. A brilliant theologian who just couldn't stand how forgiving the Church was getting. Excommunicated, reconciled, and eventually canonized. Icon behavior. The only antipope with a feast day.

3. **Clement VII (1378–1394)** Backed by France, Scotland, Aragon, and Naples—half of Europe thought he was the real pope during the Western Schism. Had the palace, the court, and the robes to back it up. His election sparked 40 years of institutional chaos.

4. **Felix V (1439–1449)** Chosen by the Council of Basel as a "compromise pope" after a democratic-style crisis. Was actually the Duke of Savoy—wealthy, powerful, and respected. Resigned gracefully when the schism ended. The HR-approved antipope.

5. Novatian (251–258) Schismatic, yes—but serious, educated, and genuinely concerned about doctrine. His beef? That the Church was letting sinners back in too easily. He was the "no second chances" pope, and his theological writings were good enough that later Church fathers quoted them (just not under his name).

TOP 5 LEAST CONVINCING ANTIPOPES

The "I Declare Myself Pope... in Kansas" Edition

1. **Benedict XIV (Jean Carrier) (1430–c. 1437)** Elected by a "conclave" of one person: himself. Had no supporters, no territories, and no credibility. Died in prison after declaring himself pope when his previously elected antipope (Benedict XIV/Garnier) died. The only person to be both the entire College of Cardinals and the pope simultaneously.

2. **Pope Michael (1990–2022)** Elected by six people in a Kansas farmhouse (including his parents). Earnest and devout, but not exactly apostolic succession material. Lived as pope for 32 years from rural Kansas with a website and YouTube presence. Gets points for longevity and sincerity, loses points for basically everything else.

3. **Constantine II (767–768)** Installed by force by his brother, a Roman duke. Wasn't even a cleric—he was ordained through all church ranks in under a week. Ruled for about a year, then was blinded, imprisoned, and had his tongue cut out. A cautionary tale in why armed takeovers rarely work in ecclesiastical politics.

4. **The Palmarian Popes (1978–Present)** Claimed that Christ transferred the papacy to Spain after Vatican II. Invented new dogmas,

banned the internet, canonized Franco, and excommunicated the entire planet except their own members. Still active, still baffling.

5. Philip (768) Proclaimed pope for one day, then went back to his monastery. Either the smartest or least ambitious antipope in history. Sometimes knowing when to quit is the real wisdom.

Honorable Mention: **Adalbert (1101)** - May not have existed at all. If he did, he left literally no trace. Being so obscure that historians debate your existence is a special achievement.

NAME THAT POPE: BEST & WORST ANTIPOPE NAMES

With honorable mentions for sheer audacity.

BEST

1. **Felix V** – Smooth. Reassuring. Sounds like a benevolent Roman uncle who gives good advice.

2. **Callixtus III** – Recycled a real pope name before it became fashionable. Elegant and symmetrical.

3. **Clement VII** – Stylish, memorable, easily confused with the real one. Perfect for a schism.

4. **Paschal III** – Bonus points for sounding like a Vatican dessert special or a particularly fancy Easter celebration.

5. **Victor IV** – Manifesting the outcome he wanted. Confident. Unfortunately there were two of them, which caused confusion.

WORST

1. **Pope Michael** – Strong name... for your high school principal. Not very papal.

2. John VIII (antipope) – Not only an antipope, but constantly confused with the legitimate Pope John VIII who came later. Historical identity theft.

3. Gregory XVII (Palmarian) – Claimed by the Palmarian pope who declared all previous popes invalid. Why stop at 17?

4. Benedict XIV (x2) – Used twice by the same mini-schism movement. Once by Garnier, once by Carrier. Very confusing.

5. Constantine II – Sounds impressive until you learn he wasn't Constantine I, and there was no legitimate Constantine pope before him. False advertising.

Honorable Mention for Confusion: Innocent III (antipope) – Shares a name with one of the most powerful popes in history (the real Innocent III, 1198-1216). The contrast is brutal: one launched crusades and crowned emperors, the other died in a monastery after a year.

WHAT THE SAINTS SAID

Mini-quotes & anecdotes from saints who fought (or forgave) antipopes

St. Catherine of Siena to Pope Gregory XI during the Avignon Papacy: "Be a manly man and not a timorous child."

Translation: Get back to Rome already and stop hiding in Avignon. Catherine didn't do subtle.

St. Vincent Ferrer, who supported Antipope Benedict XIII for years... Initially believed Benedict XIII was the legitimate pope and preached on his behalf throughout Europe. But when Benedict refused to step down even after all his supporters abandoned him, Vincent withdrew his support and recognized Martin V. He reportedly told Benedict's remaining followers that continuing the schism was harmful to the Church and that unity required compromise—even from those convinced of their own legitimacy.

His change of position persuaded entire kingdoms to abandon the Avignon claim and helped end the Western Schism.

St. Bernard of Clairvaux, who supported Innocent II against Antipope Anacletus II: "Anacletus has the city, but Innocent has the Church."

The spiritual mic drop of the 12th century. Bernard mobilized European support for Innocent through sheer rhetorical force, though his attacks on Anacletus's Jewish ancestry were among the ugliest aspects of the campaign.

Cardinal Pierre d'Ailly (not a canonized saint, but a major Church thinker during the Western Schism): "The bark of Peter cannot have two helms."

Said during his push to end the schism through the Council of Constance. A poetic way of saying "we need one pope, people."

St. Antoninus of Florence, reflecting on the Western Schism: "There were two popes, both elected, both accepted, both powerful, both held as true by many. But the Church can only have one head."

A calm theological observation and a reminder of how destabilizing divided papal claims could be—even when both claimants had legitimate arguments.

TOP 5 WEIRDEST PAPAL ELECTIONS

Because sometimes "habemus papam" came after chaos, coercion, or combat.

1. The Mob Rule Election (366 AD) When Pope Liberius died, two factions in Rome held simultaneous elections. Damasus I and Antipope Ursinus both claimed victory—followed by riots, street fights, and over 100 deaths in a single day at the Basilica of St. Mary Major. Less "sacred conclave," more "urban warfare with bishops."

2. The Three-Pope Election (1046) There were three competing popes (Benedict IX, Sylvester III, and Gregory VI) when Henry III of Germany showed up and said, "We're rebooting the whole system." He forced all three to resign and handpicked Clement II. Problem solved —through imperial diktat.

3. The One-Week Ordination Marathon (767) Constantine II wasn't a priest, deacon, or even in minor orders. Solution? His brother Duke Toto had him ordained through every ecclesiastical rank in under a week, then crowned him pope. Speed-running the priesthood didn't help—Constantine was later blinded and imprisoned.

4. The Avignon Doubleheader (1378) Urban VI was elected in Rome—but under pressure and surrounded by a hostile mob demanding an Italian pope. Soon after, French cardinals declared the election invalid and elected Clement VII in Avignon. The Western Schism was born from fear, mob pressure, and buyer's remorse.

5. Pope Michael's Basement Conclave (1990) Six people, one farmhouse in Kansas, zero cardinals. One papal election. If you ever feel underqualified, remember: David Bawden got the job and held it for 32 years. Location: Belvue, Kansas. Participants: Six, including his parents. Outcome: One of the longest-serving modern antipopes.

TOP 5 SCHISM CLEAN-UP CREWS

Heroes (and institutions) that finally said: "Okay, enough."

1. The Council of Constance (1414–1418) The Church had three rival popes. Constance deposed or pressured all of them out, elected Martin V, and told everyone to please calm down. The most productive ecclesiastical HR meeting in history. Ended the Western Schism after 40 years of chaos.

2. St. Vincent Ferrer Initially backed Benedict XIII (Avignon line), then switched sides when Benedict refused to resign for the good of the Church. His defection persuaded entire kingdoms to abandon the Avignon claim and helped tip the balance toward unity.

3. Sigismund, Holy Roman Emperor Literally dragged rival popes to the negotiating table and told them they weren't leaving until someone gave up the tiara. Papal diplomacy, imperial style. Convened the Council of Constance and enforced its decisions.

4. St. Catherine of Siena Her letters to Gregory XI helped pressure him to leave Avignon and return to Rome in 1377. She didn't resolve the schism directly, but she definitely lit the match that burned down the Avignon papacy. Died before the Western Schism began, but her push for Roman restoration was crucial.

5. The Actual Popes Who Stepped Aside Pope Gregory XII gets special mention for resigning in 1415 for the good of the Church—becoming the last pope to resign until Benedict XVI in 2013. His willingness to give up power helped end the Western Schism. Also, Felix V (1449) for resigning gracefully instead of clinging to a hopeless claim.

TOP 5 PETTIEST PAPAL MOVES DURING SCHISMS

Because when your rival claims the Chair of Peter, sometimes you get petty.

1. **Mutual Excommunications** Clement VII and Urban VI kicked off the Western Schism by excommunicating each other. Nothing says "one holy catholic church" like a theological slap-fight with eternal consequences.

2. **New Cardinals for Everybody** Both camps during the Western Schism created entirely new batches of cardinals, just to stack the deck in future elections. It was like a loyalty program for schismatic allegiance. By the end, there were so many cardinals that nobody knew who was legitimate.

3. **Two of Everything** Two papal courts, two sets of bishops, two lines of succession. Even two versions of sainthood—some saints were canonized by one pope and rejected by the other. The Schism basically created Catholic Church: Multiplayer Mode.

4. **Avignon: Papal Capital or Papal Airbnb?** Clement VII set up an entire papal palace in Avignon as a rival Rome—complete with gilded halls, extensive vineyards, and a surprisingly good wine list. If you're going to schism, at least do it in comfort.

5. Public Papal Smack-Talk Antipopes and popes both issued official proclamations calling each other usurpers, heretics, and false shepherds. Bulls flying back and forth like medieval Twitter threads. Spiritual maturity, 14th-century edition.

MOST FORGOTTEN ANTIPOPES

Even Church historians need to Google these.

1. Adalbert (1101) Historians aren't even sure this guy existed. If he did, he made so little impact that he's often considered a clerical error—literally. Possibly the only antipope created by accident through bad record-keeping.

2. Theodore (687) May have been elected pope... for a few hours. Or maybe claimed he was. Either way, he blinked and disappeared from the historical record. Part of the chaotic three-way split with Sergius I and Paschal.

3. Philip (768) Installed by forces (possibly Lombard, possibly confused Roman clergy) for a single day, then went back to his monastery. His reign lasted approximately one morning. Smart man.

4. Boniface VII (974 & 984–985) Twice declared pope, twice exiled. Died in suspicious circumstances with a hoard of stolen Vatican treasure. The Church tried to pretend he never happened. His corpse was dragged through the streets by angry Romans.

5. Christopher (903–904?) May have been a valid pope... then maybe not. His name was on official lists for centuries until someone quietly deleted it in the 20th century. Ghosted by history. Even his legitimacy is uncertain.

BEST ANTIPOPE COMEBACKS

Because some of these guys had main-character energy.

1. Hippolytus (c. 217–235) History's first antipope... who eventually reconciled with the Church, died a martyr, and was canonized. The only antipope to pull the ultimate Uno reverse card. Has a feast day. You can't top that.

2. Anacletus II (1130–1138) Backed by most of Rome, majority of cardinals, and powerful noble families. Even St. Bernard had to bring out the theological big guns to unseat him. He didn't win—but he held Rome for eight years and created a kingdom that lasted centuries. He made them work for it.

3. Felix V (1439–1449) Last major antipope. Reigned for 10 years, appointed real cardinals, then gracefully resigned and became a bishop again. Respectfully acknowledged defeat and got to retire as a duke. Probably the best exit strategy of any antipope.

4. Benedict XIII (1394–1423) Refused to resign even after everyone abandoned him—including his own cardinals and the king who originally backed him. Held out in a castle, issuing papal decrees to no one. Never say die. Literally died still claiming to be pope at age 95.

5. Clement VII (1378–1394) Controlled Avignon and half of Europe. For many Catholics at the time, he was the real pope for decades. A reminder that winning the narrative can be just as powerful as winning the vote. Created a fully functional rival papacy that required a council to dismantle.

SCHISMATICS WHO SHOULD'VE SAT DOWN AND BEEN QUIET

History's loudest theological wrong turns.

1. **Novatian (251–258)** Brilliant theologian... who thought the Church was too soft on sinners. His solution? A purist sect that broke off permanently. The Church responded by carrying on without him for 1,700 years. His movement lasted about a century before fading.

2. **Benedict XIII (1394–1423)** Refused to resign for three decades. Even after everyone left—including St. Vincent Ferrer and the king of Aragon—he held court in a Spanish fortress with one cardinal. Died in exile, still pope in his own head. Stubbornness: 10/10. Political awareness: 0/10.

3. **Urban VI (1378–1389)** Technically the real pope, but his paranoia and violent behavior helped spark the Western Schism. Sometimes being right isn't enough—you also have to not alienate literally everyone. His harsh treatment of cardinals drove them to elect Clement VII.

4. **Anacletus II (1130–1138)** Had the wealth, the Roman nobility, and majority of cardinals behind him—but still lost. Modern historians debate his legitimacy, but at the time, Bernard of Clairvaux's propaganda campaign and his Jewish ancestry doomed his papacy despite strong electoral backing.

5. Any Modern YouTube Pope If your papacy fits in a TikTok bio or you're making papal announcements from a recliner—consider taking up model trains instead. The internet has created more self-declared popes than all previous centuries combined.

FINAL THOUGHTS

Or, A Papal Epilogue for the Spiritually Curious and Historically Conflicted

So, what have we learned?

That history is messier than doctrine. That the keys to the kingdom have, at times, been duplicated, misplaced, or jammed into the wrong door entirely. That for every Peter, there's a Philip (even if only for 24 hours). And that even in the most holy institutions, humans will still be humans—with egos, ambitions, and the occasional tiara tantrum.

But maybe that's why the story matters.

Because the Church survived. Through schisms, scandals, and schismatic scandals.

Through emperors who thought they were popes, popes who thought they were emperors, and antipopes who thought they were both.

Through Anacletus II holding Rome for eight years with majority cardinal support. Through Benedict XIII refusing to quit even when down to one supporter. Through a three-pope crisis that required a council to sort out. Through Pope Michael being elected in a Kansas farmhouse.

And yes—some of these would-be pontiffs were pious. Some were political. A few were clearly off their rockers. But all of them—every last one—played a part in shaping what we now call Church history.

In the end, this isn't just a catalog of chaos. It's a mirror of our own contradictions: faith and fallibility, authority and absurdity, conviction and confusion. Because if the story of the papacy is one of divine continuity...

...then the story of the antipapacy is one of very human interruption.

And what's history, really, if not one long struggle between the two?

So go forth, dear reader—blessed with better trivia, sharper dinner party anecdotes, and a deeper appreciation for how strange and resilient the Church has always been.

And if someone ever tells you they're the true pope?

Ask for a footnote.

GLOSSARY OF TERMS

Anathema A formal curse or condemnation issued by Church authority. The theological equivalent of being very loudly and very officially unfriended. Usually meant excommunication plus extra emphasis.

Antipope A person who claims to be pope in opposition to the one officially recognized by the Catholic Church. Sometimes backed by kings and councils—sometimes just by vibes and a website.

Apostolic See A term for the papal office rooted in the belief that the Bishop of Rome is the direct successor of Saint Peter. The office many wanted. Only one (at a time) should have had.

Avignon Papacy (1309–1377) The period when the pope resided in Avignon, France instead of Rome. Critics called it exile; France called it convenient. Set the stage for the Western Schism.

Canon Law The legal system of the Catholic Church. The rulebook for everything from heresy trials to papal elections. Think: courtroom drama, but with incense.

Cardinal A senior Church official (usually a bishop) who advises the pope and elects his successor. Also known to occasionally form schism-friendly voting blocs.

Claimant Someone who asserts their right to the papacy—without full canonical or political support. See also: hopefuls, rebels, and extremely confident Kansans.

Conciliarism The belief that a general Church council holds authority over the pope in times of crisis. Popular during schism years. Not so popular at the Vatican today. Led to Felix V's election.

Council A formal gathering of Church leaders to resolve disputes or define doctrine. Sometimes helpful. Sometimes chaotic. Sometimes both. (See: Council of Pisa, which made the schism worse.)

Council of Constance (1414–1418) The council that ended the Western Schism by deposing or accepting the resignations of all rival popes and electing a new one. Possibly the most successful HR intervention in history.

Deposition The removal of a pope or antipope from office—sometimes through a council, sometimes via political muscle, and sometimes because enough people were simply tired of the drama.

Election (Papal) The process by which a pope is chosen, typically by the College of Cardinals. Historically not always peaceful or transparent. Sometimes involved bribery, intimidation, or literal brawls.

Excommunication A formal ban from participating in the sacraments and community of the Church. The preferred tool for dealing with heretics, rival popes, and overambitious bishops.

Holy Roman Empire A political entity in central Europe that frequently inserted itself into papal affairs. Not particularly holy, Roman, or an empire by the end—but very good at backing antipopes.

Imperial Investiture The act of secular rulers (like emperors) appointing church officials. A major source of conflict that fueled many papal schisms and anti-papal adventures throughout the Middle Ages.

Investiture Controversy The 11th-12th century conflict over whether secular rulers or the Church had the right to appoint bishops. Produced numerous antipopes and reshaped Church-state relations. Resolved (sort of) by the Concordat of Worms in 1122.

Legitimacy The recognition of a pope's rightful claim to office. Often clarified after the fact—when historians and Church leaders finally agree on who was actually pope.

Papal Bull A formal decree issued by the pope. Often used to make sweeping declarations, excommunicate rivals, or remind everyone who's in charge. Named after the lead seal (bulla) attached to the document.

Papal Court The central administration of the pope. Antipopes often set up their own rival courts—with competing officials, bishops, and sometimes nicer wine.

Papal Primacy The doctrine that the pope has supreme authority over the entire Church. A key point of contention in many schisms and rebellions.

Resignation (Papal) A rare but canonically possible act. Only a few popes (and even fewer antipopes) have resigned. Most had to be nudged—or removed. Gregory XII (1415) and Felix V (1449) both resigned to end schisms.

Rival Claim A competing assertion of papal authority. Sometimes based on theology. Often based on politics. Occasionally based on "I had a vision."

Roman Curia The administrative and judicial institutions that help the pope govern the Church. Sometimes loyal. Sometimes divided during schisms.

Schism A formal break in communion—usually involving rival popes, disputed elections, and decades of awkward ecclesiastical silence.

Sede Vacante Latin for "the seat being vacant." Refers to the time between papacies. Occasionally used (or abused) by claimants to justify new elections.

Sedevacantism The belief that the current pope is not valid and that the Holy See is vacant. A favorite theological framework for modern papal fringe groups. Claims the last valid pope died decades ago (date varies by group).

Tiara (Papal) The ceremonial triple crown worn by popes (and some antipopes) in past centuries. A towering symbol of authority, unity... and flair. No longer used regularly, but still iconic.

Usurpation Illegitimately claiming an office or title—like the papacy—without proper authority. The preferred pastime of many an ambitious cleric.

Vatican The independent city-state and spiritual HQ of the Catholic Church. Also, the place where most people now agree the pope lives. (Usually.)

Western Schism (1378–1417) A period when two—and later three—rival claimants declared themselves pope. A theological standoff with very real political consequences. The defining papal crisis of the late Middle Ages.

SUGGESTED FURTHER READING & RESOURCES

For readers who want to go deeper—or just double-check that we didn't make this all up—here are some essential sources:

BOOKS

***Pope Culture: Fun Facts, Scandals & Mini Bios of Every Pope in History* by Pamela Pettyfeather**

The companion book to this one! Shorter bios; hilarious trivia lists. Pope-apalooza. Real papal history with a wink, in bite-sized chunks. Much more fun than the books below. ;-)

***Saints and Sinners: A History of the Popes* by Eamon Duffy**

A smart, readable history of the papacy—warts, tiaras, and all. Covers both legitimate popes and their rivals with historical clarity and engaging prose.

***The Oxford Dictionary of Popes* by J.N.D. Kelly & Michael Walsh**

Still the gold standard for quick bios on every pope and antipope.

Comprehensive, well-researched, and essential for anyone studying papal history.

Vicars of Christ: A History of the Popes **by Charles A. Coulombe**

Narrative-driven and often traditionalist in tone, but rich with colorful detail and interesting perspectives on papal history.

BONUS POPE CULTURE PUZZLE PACK

Test your pope knowledge with a printable Pope-pourri of puzzles based on *Pope Culture* & *Antipope Culture*!

Free for all purchasers of *Pope Culture* or *Antipope* Culture; it's total brain-teasery fun!

Scan the QR code above!

(E-book readers can click here to access it!)

ACKNOWLEDGMENTS

To the historians who've spent careers untangling papal numbering schemes and debating whether Christopher was ever really pope.

To the archivists who've preserved centuries of bulls, counter-bulls, and excommunications—even the embarrassing ones.

To St. Hippolytus, for being reconciled and reminding us that even first antipopes can become saints.

To Anacletus II, for holding out for eight years and creating a kingdom that outlasted his condemnation by seven centuries.

To Benedict XIII, for showing us what stubbornness looks like when taken to its absolute limit.

To Pope Michael and all the modern claimants, for keeping the tradition alive in the strangest possible ways.

To the Council of Constance, for actually fixing the unfixable.

And to every reader who made it through 45+ antipopes without losing track of which Benedict was which—you're the real heroes here.

This book exists because antipopes refuse to be forgotten, even when the Church tries very hard to forget them.

May we all be so persistently memorable.

POPE CULTURE

"Okay, real talk...*Pope Culture* by Pamela Pettyfeather is one of the most random but entertaining books I've read in a while. I didn't expect to get sucked into a book about popes, but here we are."

- GinnyR @ Amazon

FROM SAINTS TO SCOUNDRELS—MEET ALL 267 POPES IN ONE HOLY HILARIOUS BOOK.

Popes have excommunicated emperors, led armies, blessed animals, and survived assassination attempts. Some were saints. Others... not so much.

Pope Culture: Fun Facts, Scandals & Mini Bios of Every Pope in History is your all-access guide to 2,000 years of papal drama—with bite-sized bios, bizarre trivia, scandalous stories, and more than a few tiaras.

QUIZ: WHICH ANTIPOPE ARE YOU?

A Heretically Irreverent Personality Quiz

From Righteous Reformer to Full-Blown Pretender: **Discover Your Inner Antipope!**

Scan the QR code above (**ebook readers click here**) to take the quiz and unlock your **FREE *Pope Culture* Puzzle Pack**!

Printed in Dunstable, United Kingdom

74337756R00096